War Time Women

True Stories by Michael Bentinck

CONTENTS

Published by Michael Bentinck © 1998

Typeset in New Baskerville
and printed on environmentally-friendly paper
by Print-Out, Histon, Cambridge, UK

ISBN 0 9526157 5 4

Front cover illustration:
Topsy Price of Ross on Wye at work on a Chepstow Farm

INTRODUCTION

The book you are about to read is full of true war time stories, just like my other books "MY DAD MY HERO", "FORGOTTEN HEROES" and " A WILL TO LIVE", which so many of you have read and have taken the time to write to me about and to express your thanks by saying just how true to life they really are, in the way they tell the true stories of my own father and his brave comrades, who gave and suffered so much at the hands of the Japanese in that horrific war for them. As so many of you have said, you too were caught up in that nightmare. In this book it is our brave ladies' true stories that are told and may I say what a privilege it has been for me to meet so many of you in your own homes and to sit and hear your wonderful stories. To be allowed to be the one to write them for you in this book really is a great honour. Once again the last section of the book is a letters section – letters that all tell a true story of what you brave ladies did in your dig for victory. Some of these letters are really amusing, and after writing my other books it was good this time to be able to have a laugh instead of shedding tears, when my emotions ran high at the thought of my dear father suffering so much. I hope, like me, you will find all the stories in this book of great interest, for they cover all walks of life and above all they show the part the ladies played in World War II.

At the time of writing this book so much is being said about "GIRL POWER" and most of you will have heard of the Spice Girls, and of how they feel about girl power. It was good to see them putting their voices to help the Royal British Legion's Poppy Appeal this Remembrance Day (1997), and I hope every young person followed their lead and wore their poppies with pride. I hope when I receive letters about this book, that one of the five Spice Girls has taken the trouble to write with their views, and yes I hope they will see that girl power was in so much demand in World War II.

It is my hope that through the sales of this book, my wife Hilary and I will be able to raise funds to help with research into breast cancer, for it has been an horrific killer in our family, and as this book is dedicated to ladies, I can't think of a better cause to help. So thank you all for your support.

DEDICATION

This book is dedicated to ladies everywhere who played their part for King and country in World War II. It does not matter whether they worked on the land, in the factories, in the hospitals, or were doing their bit in His Majesty's Service. I want them to know that they are not forgotten and that we really do appreciate the part they played in giving us younger ones our today. In my research for this book, I heard from many ladies who lost a friend while doing their part for the war effort. To lay down one's life for their fellow man is really the greatest sacrifice that anyone can make, and as we have read in my other books, "MY DAD MY HERO", "FORGOTTEN HEROES" and "A WILL TO LIVE", so many brave souls did just that in World War II. So, as I say, this book is dedicated to our brave "WAR TIME WOMEN" and to the memory of all those who gave their lives for our today. (May they rest in Peace).

ACKNOWLEDGEMENTS

My thanks go to all the wonderful ladies who have shared their War Time Stories with me, and have therefore made this book possible. I will not name them all here for their names appear in the book with their stories. I also thank the many ladies who wrote to me wanting their stories told of their wartime experiences. As you will see, I have used some of these in the letters section of the book. The many others I have kept on file, for if this book does well and you my readers enjoy it, then it will be my pleasure to write another. I also thank my friend and presenter from BBC Radio Cambridgeshire, Mandy Morton, for giving me the idea to write a book of true stories of "WAR TIME WOMEN".

So many of you have written to say how much you enjoy the programmes that Mandy and I do together on this subject. I thank all the friends I have made across our great Country who work for the BBC Radio stations, for allowing me to do wartime programmes for them. I thank my editor, Mike Johnson, and his team at Print-Out U.K. (my publishers) for all their help and expertise. Also my dear wife Hilary, for all her help and support, for thanks to her, I can always tell if we have received another moving letter from one of you, as she sits crying as she reads the letter, or if it is an amusing letter, of course she can't stop laughing. This way I know whether to put it on the happy or sad pile of letters. Also I thank my own Spice Girl, Mrs. Ruby Spice, of Kent, for the kindness and friendship that she and her husband Jim have shown to Hilary and I. Ruby ordered and paid for this book before I had even put pen to paper!

My special thanks go to actress Kathy Staff, better known to you all as Nora Batty in the BBC Television serial "Last of the Summer Wine", for the wonderful foreword that she has written for this book. Kathy is a lady who knows all about World War Two, and of how wars affect ordinary families. I would recommend to you Kathy's book, "MY STORY – WRINKLES AND ALL".

Last, but certainly not least, my thanks to you my readers, for without you, I could not begin to help with donations towards the ongoing research into Breast Cancer.

FOREWORD

by Kathy Staff

It is indeed a great privilege to be asked to write the foreword for this wonderful book of true stories which show how we ladies played our part in World War Two for King and Country. As you will see through the course of the book, women had to be jacks-of-all-trades to keep our great country going while so many of our men were away fighting for our today. And when the War was won, it was still left to the ladies to help make our country great again, as our brave men returning from war – in many cases from prison camps in Europe and the Far East – had to be fed and cared for until they could fit back into a normal life, if life could ever be normal for them again!

Michael shows us with such feeling the wonderful job these ladies did in feeding and providing for us in those dark days of World War Two. They, like so many others of that time, are all unsung heroes, and I thank Michael for recording these true stories for us and future generations.

As many of you will know, the success of Michael's other books has enabled him to help with donations towards the Far Eastern Prisoners of War. It pleased me to learn that through the sales of this book, donations will be made to breast cancer research. As this is a book of ladies experiences, I cannot think of a more worthwhile cause. I hope, like me, you will find these stories enjoyable and of great interest.

Kathy Staff.

Marion Andrews' Story

The story you are about to read is the true story of Marion Andrews and I am privileged that she has shared her story with me and has allowed me to share it with you now.

I shall never forget the first time I met Marion. It was Sunday 10th August 1997. I had spoken with her on the 'phone and we had written to one another a few times after Marion had heard a programme I did for BBC Radio Kent with my dear presenter friend Barbara Sturgeon. The programme concentrated on wartime stories of my father and his comrades who suffered such horrific treatment at the hands of the Japanese in World War II. Barbara asked me what my next book would be about, and I was pleased to be able to say that it would be a book of true stories of what ladies did for King and country during the war. I asked on the programme that if any ladies had a story they wanted to be told in the book, to please make contact with me and thankfully Marion did just that.

We arranged that my wife Hilary and I would visit her on 10th August. It was a very hot day and the journey took us about 2½ hours plus another half an hour to find Great Lathe Farm, Burmarsh – Marion's home. As we drew into the large car park, my wife and I knew we were to meet a very special lady for we could see a shop that said "Grans Shop" plus large tea rooms that served all manner of wonderful food including cream teas and fresh strawberries, which started my mouth watering straight away. There is also a large farm museum which really is a tribute to all Land Army girls and all farm workers of that era. There is also a Pets Corner that is a must for all ages to see – baby rabbits, cattle, barn owls, peacocks, ducks and geese, turkeys, etc. etc. – the only thing we didn't see was a unicorn. The donkey and pony did just as well though, and we could tell that we really were down on the farm.

After a brief look round we went to Marion's house and knocked on the door. I think she had guessed who we were and shouted for us to come in. She greeted us as if we had known one another for years and straight away wanted to make us tea and something to eat. She took us through to her lounge and sat me down then gave me all her notes and photos of her time in the Land Army. She said "now you sit and look through that lot while Hilary and I go and make us a drink and *something to eat". As I sat looking through Marion's notes and photos I could tell I was in for a wonderful story – a story that I hope you will all find of great interest, for I know that many of you who will be reading it will have been Land Army girls, and will know for yourselves what hard work it was on the farms in World War II.*

When Marion and Hilary returned to the room you can imagine I had many questions to ask Marion and over the next few hours we sat chatting about the remarkable times in her life. Then before we left we were given a guided tour of the whole estate, which even has a small golf course. It is a place I would recommend to you all and I feel sure after reading Marion's story it is a place you will want to visit – and if you visit Gran's Shop whilst there, I'm sure you will get to meet Marion in person. I know that she will be pleased to chat with you for she has told me many times how much she loves meeting and talking with people.

Marion's story begins in 1921 at number 1 Rutland Villas, Ballimena, Limerick, Ireland on 14th April, the place where she was born. Her mother and father christened her Marion Annie Davis. Marion was the second child for her parents, having already had a son born on 12th March 1920, whom they called William Arthur. While Marion and William were still only babies, their mother had two more girls to make their family complete – Margaret Elizabeth on 1st March 1923, and Olive Mai on 25th June 1925. One thing they all had in common, apart from being brother and sisters, was that they were all born at 1 Rutland Villas. As Marion says "a real handful for her dear mother, especially as times were hard, for the Great War to end all wars had not long been finished" – a war that had left its scar on most families. Marion's father had done his part for King and country in this war with the Rifle Brigade in France, where he was wounded and gassed but through his brave actions he did win the Military Medal – something that Marion and her family can be so very proud of.

Marion's mother, Olive, was born in Enniskillen, Ireland in 1890 and not long after her birth her mother died so Olive was raised by her father's sister and her husband, a Mr and Mrs F Scales. They had no children of their own at this time but when Olive was 10 years old her aunt, whose name was Maggie, had a son whom they called Arthur, then 18 months later she had a second son, Frank.

The whole family were very strong Baptists and went to church three times on a Sunday, and attended bible meetings etc. twice during the week. Another family they befriended through the Chapel was the Davis family who numbered seven in all – Mr Christopher Davis, Mrs Annie Davis and their five children. One of the children, William, was to become Marion's father. Mr Christopher Davis had come over to Ireland from Spalding in Lincolnshire and had bought a printing business in Limerick. Marion's father-to-be, young William, who was born in 1884, worked in the printing shop for his father as did his brother Charlie. The other brother, the youngest of the five children, was named after his father and young Christopher would also help out when he was allowed to. The two girls, Mabel and Maria, were gifted at dressmaking and lace work and this kept them very busy.

As the two girls got older they set up their own dressmaking business. After the Great War when William came home he could not settle in the printing shop, and so he set off to work in London where he trained to be an electrician and worked on the building of the underground railway system. I would imagine that Olive had by this time fallen very much in love with William for she ran away to London to be with him. This angered her father – and her aunt and uncle, who would have no more to do with her from then on. They had brought her up very strictly and would not let her out of their sight unless it was to attend a meeting at the Baptist Chapel. I dare say that Olive told them she was off to a chapel meeting the day she ran away to London. She found her dear William and on the 26th December 1918 they were married. Soon after the wedding Olive was feeling so homesick mixed with a sense of guilt for what she had put her father through. As you can imagine, she was his life after losing his wife soon after she was born. So William brought her home to Limerick where they rented a little house – yes, number 1 Rutland Villas, the home where their children were to be born. Olive's father, Mr James Greer, a retired policeman, also came to live with them and found himself a job at Denny's Bacon Factory in Limerick so that he could help his daughter and her new husband for times were so very hard and he knew that every penny that came into the house would be needed.

By this time William's mother and father and his two sisters had moved to Bedford in England to a house in Foster Hill Road, number 196, leaving the two other boys to run the printing business. Here the two girls set up their dressmaking business, again in one of the large bedrooms in the house at Foster Hill Road. They were kept very busy here making dresses for the wives and children of Army Officers' before they set off to India with their husbands and their regiments.

Back in Ireland soon after the birth of Olives last child, young Olive Mai, in 1925, William knew he had to find better paid work so that he could support the family. He managed to get a job with the Westinghouse Brake and Signal company in England. Little Olive Mai was only two months old at this time. William soon missed his family very badly, so he brought them all over to England. He had managed to save enough money to buy a house in Edenthorpe, Yorkshire, for a cost of £300 which in 1925 was a small fortune to a working class man.

Before they all left Ireland they were visited by Olive's aunt and uncle, the ones who would have nothing to do with her when she ran away to be with William. Yet here they were on the very day that Olive and the family were to leave. They were in tears and said "we can't let you leave again without telling you just how much we miss you", and after lots of crying and cuddling, they were once again the best of friends, and would remain so for the rest of their days. (Thank God that their real Christian love overcame their anger).

After the family arrived in England and made the long trip up to Yorkshire, all Marion and her brother and sisters wanted to do was get to bed, for they were so tired – but as they arrived at the house, their poor father could see that the builders hadn't finished, and it was certainly nowhere near ready to live in. A kindly neighbour took them all in and this was Marion's first sight of farming, for the lady ran a smallholding. Marion remembers that there were chickens everywhere. She also sold old house furniture from a large garden shed which many of the villagers were glad of at that time when setting up home. Marion and her family stayed with this good neighbour for two months until their own house was ready. Marion recalled the first time she entered 5 Conisboro Road, Edenthorpe – "it was only a three bedroomed semi, but it seemed like a mansion to me. We even had a bathroom downstairs and a kitchen. We had a living room and a lounge (or best room as we called it, for we were only allowed in it if we had posh company visit us). We had no electricity so had to use oil lamps, but it was my first home in England and the people were so kind that to this day I have happy memories of my time there".

By this time her brother, William Arthur, known to all as Billy, was of school age but the school he was asked to attend was at Armthorpe, which, even going across the fields, was about three miles away – not too good for a boy of five years old. Once a week a lady called Mrs Singleton came round in a large old lorry from which she sold all manner of things such as pots and pans, and oil for the lamps. "My mother asked her if she knew of a school that had a bus service. Mrs Singleton told her that where she lived, at Hatfield Woodhouse, there was a very nice school and buses passed it every half hour. Mother then made arrangements for Billy and I to start school together when I was five, which meant that Billy never started school until he was six. We would catch the Premier bus every morning at 8.30am and catch one home at 3.45pm. We had a weekly bus pass that cost mum about two shillings a week".

By the time their two sisters Margaret Elizabeth (known as Betty) and young Olive Mai were ready to start school, a mission hall had been built in Edenthorpe and this was used for the children until they were 11 years old. It was also used for Sunday school and church on Sundays so Marion and her brother and sisters spent six days a week here.

The village was growing fast now with new houses springing up all over the place – a new post office opened, plus two shops and, yes, a fish and chip shop, a thing all children seem to remember with affection. As the village continued to grow they even had their own milkman and Marion recalled with such happiness her memories of his horse and cart, for she would often be the one to go out to him with the milk jug for him to fill from his churns, and of course she always took something out for his horse to eat. She did the same for the coal man when he delivered their coal. All the children loved to see and feed the horses.

Marion remembered that the baker came round on his large delivery bike with his large basket on the front. She would buy 13 of his lovely buns (a bakers dozen). She told me with a smile, that once her brothers and sisters joined her the buns were soon gone. It really was a lovely place to live and it was good for Marion to grow up seeing these lovely working horses. In the years to come, she too would find them of great help.

Marion's father William was now working for the main Hatfield coal pit as well as some of the others around the area. His knowledge of electrical works and of working underground were invaluable in the mines, for he had learnt well during the time he worked on the London underground. Marion and the rest of the family never saw much of him as he was always working, but he provided well for them and when he was with them he did his best to amuse them. In 1928, on Marion's seventh birthday, she found herself very ill with bronchial pneumonia. She never left the house for nearly three months, and remembered that at the beginning of the illness she was so ill she just lay in bed and slept. Every time she opened her eyes there were Easter eggs at the foot of her bed but she was too ill to eat them. Of course there were not the drugs like we have today, so it was a long time before Marion was up and about again.

Once well and back at school she soon caught up with her work, for she enjoyed school, unlike her brother Billy, who would rather be helping the village farmers and earning himself a bob or two. Marion loved sports days and would take part in all the races she could. When Rose Queen day came she was only too pleased to take part. Her mother Olive always came to watch her and gave support in anything that any of her children took part in at the school.

One day while out playing with her brother Billy, some of the other village boys who were playing with them in one of the farmers meadows, dared them to set light to an old haystack that had fallen down. As there were cattle in the meadow Billy and Marion said they would not, but, children being children, they would not stop their jibes and said "just 'cos you lot are better off than us you daren't do anything, you goody goodies". This angered Billy and Marion and they replied "if the cows weren't here we would". The other children replied "well they won't be here first thing Saturday morning – they'll be being milked so you'd better be here first thing and bring some matches or you're scaredy cats".

So on Saturday morning after breakfast, Marion and Billy went off to meet the others at the meadow. It was a fine hot morning and you can imagine the taunts coming from the other children so Marion lit her match and held it to a small bit of straw that stuck out of the side of the old haystack. Within seconds the whole stack was ablaze, and the children were off like a shot, jumping over the fence to the meadow and away home. One of the older villagers must have noticed the fire for in no time at all the Fire Brigade and Police were on the scene.

It was not long before they knocked on Marion and Billy's door. Young Billy didn't wait – he was up and off to his bedroom where he hid himself under his bed. As their mother let the police in, Marion's heart was in her mouth, such was her fear of the ordeal to come. She answered the policeman's questions – of course she knew nothing about it. Her and Billy had not left the house! Billy wouldn't come out of his room, so never did speak with the policeman. Things soon blew over and they heard no more about it until months later when they heard that the farmer was pleased it had been set alight, as it was only a load of old rubbish covered over with straw and whoever did it had saved him the job of moving it!

Marion told me that the other children thought them to be well off as their father was an electrician, while their fathers were miners and farm labourers, and looking back she tells me they probably *were* that little better off than most at that time. She remembered that every Saturday the postman brought a registered letter for mother which contained housekeeping that dad had sent her. It was always four £1 notes.

Their house at Edenthorpe was always an open house for Olive. Marion's mother loved company and they would have a real housefull when the aunt and uncle who brought up Olive came over from Ireland, for they would bring with them their two boys, plus grandad and grandmother from Bedford, and the two girls would come (the ones that had the dressmaking business). It would be a real housefull but to young Marion it was a time of great excitement with so many of her relations to spoil her.

At school they had started up the Yorkshire penny bank and every Monday morning the children who could afford it took a penny to school to save in the bank. Marion's little bank book soon built up as did her brother and sisters' books and when their mother took them home to Ireland for a holiday this saving was a godsend and helped them to have a wonderful time.

Marion also loved it when she went to stay with her grandad and grandmother at Bedford and if she could get into her aunt's bedroom-cum-workroom she loved to dress up in all the fine clothes that they made for the well-to-do ladies who were off to India. Marion and her sisters would pretend that they were also very rich ladies once they were dressed in all the finery. Such wonderful childhood memories are priceless but come Sunday it all changed – no playing was allowed; it was church in the morning and again at night, with Sunday school at 3.00pm in the afternoon. You had to wear your best clothes all that day and woe betide you if you got them dirty for grandad and grandma Davis were very strict, especially on Sundays.

Marion's father was offered a very good job at this time – the only trouble was that it was in Brazil! The whole family were planning to go and it was to be a great adventure for Marion and her brother and sisters. It was now 1929 and father left for Brazil at once to make arrangements for them all to go over there as soon as possible. It was left to Marion's mother to put the house up for sale and to be ready to go as soon as father sent for them. Marion remembered the trip to Liverpool on the train to see her father off, and they all waved to him until the ship was out of sight. Over the next couple of months the house was sold but just as the paperwork was completed and signed, word came from Brazil that a revolution had broken out and it would not be safe for them to go there, and they were to stay in England. Imagine the shock to poor Olive and the children – their dream of adventure was shattered.

As the house had been sold, they rented a house in Eden Grove in the village of Edenthorpe. By now Billy was 10 years old, Marion was 9, Betty 7 and little Olive Mai was just 5. The house they were now living in was number 10, Eden Grove. It stood opposite Edenthorpe Hall where a Scottish Lord had lived but by now much of it had been converted into flats for miners and their families to live in. It was here that Marion decided, at such a young age, that she would never touch alcohol, for the sights she saw there have stayed with her to this day. Many times on the way home from school with Billy, they would have to run in fear as chairs, knives etc. came flying out of the doorways and windows of these flats. The language of course was not for 9 and 10 year olds to hear and the sight of men beating their wives was also a despicable thing to have to see, especially for ones so young.

These events were always worse on a Friday after the miners had been paid. Many of them, instead of taking their wages home, would go for a drink which, after being below ground all week on the coal face etc., is no bad thing except that many of these men who lived in the flats never knew when to stop and so went home very drunk. When the poor wife saw them they knew from experience what they were in for. Of course, after the husbands sobered up they were full of apologies and told their wives it would never happen again, but of course the very next time the demon drink took hold of them the wife was in for the same treatment. Marion was terrified to have to walk by the flats, such was her fear of one of these men attacking her. She had seen for herself many of the children from these families at school with their black eyes and bruises. She also saw that sometimes they would come to school in new shoes or boots, then a week later not be at school at all because their father had taken them and sold them for more drinking money. Marion knew that it would have been the mother that would have scrimped and saved to get her child the new shoes and it was her and the child who always suffered. So at nine years old she made her decision never to touch alcohol and to just be tee-total.

In Hatfield Woodhouse a large estate called White City was built to house a lot of mining families. Marion told me how she will never forget the poverty that she saw at this time in her life, for the families were so poor with 9 to 11 children in most families. What chance did they have? She remembered that these dear children received free milk at school, and cod liver oil and malt etc. while she and the others paid a halfpenny for their third of a pint and two dry biscuits. Most children stayed at school for their dinner but brought their own sandwiches to eat. Many of the children were from the farms on the moors nearby and had a five mile walk to school, so by lunchtime always had a hearty appetite. Marion never forgot the sandwiches these children had – they were always red in colour and it was some time before she dare ask any of them what was in them. She soon found out that the ½" thick slices of stale bread had just slices of beetroot in them. She also remembered that the sandwiches that she had for most of her life at school contained meat paste – day in day out, always paste. On very special occasions, like her birthday, if she was lucky, she would find she had real red salmon in them and a drop of cocoa or Oxo powder which you put in your mug and then the tea monitor came round and put your hot water in for you. All the children remained sitting at their desks to have their lunch and afterwards one of the children would be given the job of sweeping up the floor and putting everything back in its place.

When the children reached 13 years old they all had a turn at being the cloakroom monitor which meant every morning, and again at dinner time, you had to make sure everywhere was tidy and wash the quarry-tiled floor. There was no hot water of course, so it was that much harder to keep clean. There were 13 W.C.'s to keep clean as well, especially the 13th one which was for the teachers' use only and if this was not kept spotless then you were for the high jump. The toilets, as you can imagine, were all old earthenware ones, and it was the job of the caretaker to empty them. Marion never did know where they were emptied – she never did see a lorry or van to take the waste away. She did know that the caretaker often won prizes for his garden produce so maybe this is where the sewage waste ended up – on the caretaker's garden.

"Once you had finished your cleaning duties, it was straight back to lessons where we had 40 to 45 children in each class. Our teachers were all very good really and looking back I can see they did the best they could for us. Our headmaster was a Mr Thompson for most of my school days and he lived in the school house next door to the school. It was from here we had to get all our water, by means of filling a bucket from the pump which was over the well in the garden. We used this water for both washing and drinking, and it was heavy work for us girls lifting buckets of water over to the school when it was your turn to wash the toilet floors etc."

"My favourite teacher was a Mr Thomas. He was so very good at geography and made it interesting for us, and of course, with my dad in Brazil, I found learning about the other countries of great interest. Mind you, if you did wrong against Mr Thomas he never was afraid to punish you, and the girls received the cane just as hard as the boys did."

"In our last few years at school mum bought us bikes, so as to save on the bus fares. These were bought from a second hand shop for about 5 shillings, and once we had these we rode the five miles to school each day up until we all left school. If any of us had received the cane from Mr Thomas it really made the bike ride home that much worse! The cheeks of your back-side would hurt so much that you could not bear them on the saddle." "Looking back it was very strict discipline. I often wonder if it would help with young offenders of today."

"One of the best days of my school life was always sports day during which I took part in as many events as I could. I remember one year my dad was home from Brazil and was asked if he would come along and present the sports day cup to the winning team. I felt very cocky having a dad who was working abroad and felt extra special when he was asked to present the cup. The next important day at school was the Rose Queen day when we had Morris dancing, sword dancing, the maypole and of course the crowning of the Rose Queen. In 1932 I was given the honour of being the school Rose Queen and was so pleased that my dad was home at the time to take some photos of me. My sister Betty was the Rose Queen the year after in 1933 – we really did feel so very important, for it really was a thing that your family could be so proud of. Soon after this my dad went to work in Poland and mum's life was about to change as well. She took in lodgers who worked at the Pilkington's Glass Factory. Soon there was not enough room so we moved again, this time to 11 Clovelly Road, a much bigger house. Soon after arriving here, my dad's sister, Aunt Mabel from Bedford, one of the dressmakers, died of breast cancer. She was just 45 years old. Billy was so very upset for she had always made it clear that he was her favourite. At the same time aunt Maggie in Ireland was taken very ill and as she had brought my mother up, mother thought she must go and care for her. We were left to fend for ourselves, but mum did arrange for a lady to come in and clean and cook for us."

"Mother stayed in Ireland for some time until her aunt had died, and to sort out all the arrangements. She then returned and brought her uncle with her. It was a very upsetting time for mother, as not long before this she had been over to make all the funeral arrangements for her own father who had stayed in Ireland when we all came over to England. So when she lost her aunt it was really like losing her parents in quick succession."

"Mum was kept so busy though, that she really didn't have a lot of time to mourn, for our house was so full of lodgers – and now so many of our relations – that once again the house was too small and so we moved again. This time it was to a very large house called White Lodge which stood in lovely large gardens. My mum's uncle was very good to us here. He had worked all his life for Guinness back in Ireland and he received a very good pension which I know he put towards the rent of this smashing house."

"At this time dad came home from Poland for three weeks, and when he went back he took Betty with him (why they ever christened her Margaret I will never know. The whole family always called her Betty). It made a wonderful time for Betty and I know she felt very privileged to have visited another country. She was brought back to England by a family that were returning to live in England. I know it was a great adventure for her. In 1934 my mother Olive and my young sister Olive Mai went to Poland and it was at this time that mum's uncle, who was now just over 65 years old, met and married a spinster who was only 45 years old. So they looked out for us while mum was away in Poland. I dare say it caused a lot of gossip around the village when my great uncle married a spinster but I know it made him very happy and of course gave him plenty to live for."

"Soon after mother returned, our village greengrocer, who had his old bedridden mother living with him, asked my mother if she knew of anyone who wanted a job helping to look after his mother and to do the housework for him. My mother replied 'my daughter Marion can do that for you', and so I was asked to leave school and start work for the greengrocer. It was now 1935 and I never wanted to leave school but mother had told him I would take the job and as she had given her word to the greengrocer, this is what I had to do."

"By now my brother Billy had gone to live with our grandparents at Bedford, where he had started an apprenticeship in engineering. Mum always wanted him to be like dad and follow in his footsteps."

"I didn't like working as a skivvy, but it was not for long, for in December 1935, on the 20th, we all moved to Bedford to live at 31 Stanley Street. After Christmas Betty and Olive Mai started school and I had to find a job. It was in the early spring of 1936 when I got a job at Mence Smiths, a large ironmongers. I can't really say that it was a job that I really wanted to do, but as they say, 'needs must'. I really wanted to be a children's nurse or a missionary but every time I mentioned this no one would take notice of me, so there I was, just another shop girl. It really was an insight into hard work, for I had to bike the three miles to work and back. My hours of work were 9.00am until 7.00pm on Monday, Tuesday and Wednesday, then 8.30am until 9.00pm Friday and Saturday. I did get a one hour lunch break and in that time I would bike home, have a quick snack and bike back again ready at my station by 2.00pm to start serving again. All this for seven shillings and six pence a week. I really did enjoy the job though, as the work was so varied. I put wicks into the customers oil lamps and stoves, I put handles on to brooms, along with selling all manner of things such as paraffin, turps, linseed oil, and chloride of lime, a thing none of us liked serving. I was working here when war broke out in 1939 and I met so many young servicemen who came into the store to buy anything from shoe laces to pots and pans. Once I had finished work for the day I would go to the Mill Street Baptist Church to help in the canteen which was open from 7.00pm until 10.00pm every night. Over cups of tea we would play cards and darts and once again I was to meet many young servicemen of all nationalities; there were Polish, Irish, Welsh, Scottish and of course English lads. We had such fun together with plenty of laughs, and as a young girl at that time I can honestly say that not one of them tried to take advantage of you – they really were all such young gentlemen. I took many of them home to meet mum and my family, but it was not long before many of them were off to fight for their countries and I was to hear no more of them. I dare say many of them were killed in action and found a grave in some foreign field. It really was a waste of such young lives, just innocent lads off to die for King and country. As if enough of them hadn't died in the First World War – yet here we were starting all over again. It makes you wonder if mankind will ever learn that war is not the answer."

"On Sunday 3 September 1939, we came out of church at 12 noon and the air raid sirens were wailing out. We at once all thought we were going to be bombed and the fear just took hold of everyone, but I am afraid it was something we were going to have to live with for years to come. It really was a treat to hear the sirens sound the all clear, when once again you would thank God that you had come through it safe and sound. Of course after the all clear had sounded, it was hard work then for the services that had to dig people out etc. and what misery it was for those dear families that lost their houses and sometimes a member of their family."

"My sister Betty was now working at Kempston Childrens' Home and Olive Mai had left school and had come to work at Mence Smiths with me. Our hours of work were still the same at this time but we had to take turns at fire watching and this meant that one night a week we would have to sleep on the shop floor, and if the sirens went we had to get up and make notes of what was happening and record it all in a large ledger. Oh how we prayed that nothing would happen and that no bombs would fall on us, for all around us were tanks of paraffin oil and turps, plus many other flammable substances. In fact, looking back, the whole premises was just a sitting time bomb. I just thank God that the German bombers never hit it on their bombing raids for there would have been nothing that I could have done to save the place – I think it fair to say I would have been burnt to death."

"Soon a large new store called Greens opened in Midland Road, which in later years became British Home Stores. One of our office girls at Mence Smiths left to work for them and soon after, I met her at the Baptist canteen one evening and she told me how good it was there and to try and get a job there myself. I remember a few days later I went for an interview and got the job, it was for 10 shillings a week and I was told if I did OK after a few weeks it would go up to 15 shillings a week, and sure enough after two weeks this is what happened. I had never been so well off. I bought a half-a-crown saving stamp each week and after my stoppages still had 11 shillings a week to take home. I gave mum 12 pence ha'penny for my keep and enjoyed the rest. I had to have a pair of stockings every week while I could get them, and they cost 4d. A pair of my shoes would cost me 3 shillings and 11 pence a pair. If there had not been a war on I think my life would have been just fine for after running a counter on my own at Mence Smiths, here I was with other girls on the same counter. I started on the hat counter but before long I was put onto the stockings and fashion counter. We were always very busy as it was not just a matter of taking the money – you had to take the dockets from the customers clothing ration book. I think I worked on every counter while employed here but none better than the mens counter. This was such good fun as the men could never get the hang of their clothing dockets. Yes, they were hopeless at working things out, and were only too glad for us girls to sort out all the paperwork for them. Many of these men were servicemen and I used to say to my workmates 'however are we going to win this war if this is anything to go by? Our men are no good at paperwork and I just hope Mr Churchill knows what he is doing.'"

"By now it was 1941 and I was now 20. I thought it was time I did my bit for my country and wondered what I could do to help the war effort. It was May and we had been having a lovely warm sunny spell, and we had a lot of girls coming into the shop who were really suntanned and looked so very well. I found out that they were in the Women's Land Army and I thought 'oh, how lovely it would be to work in the open air and not have to be in a stuffy shop all the time.' Without much thought really, I went off to the Bedford Women's Land Army office to see what I had to do about joining. Thankfully by now my dad was back in England. He had found it very hard to get out of Poland when war had been declared and for a long time we heard nothing of him, but thank God he had lived on his wits and had managed to get back safely."

"My brother Billy was in a reserved occupation but once he saw all his mates joining up and going away he decided to volunteer for the R.A.F. and after his training he got on a Sunderland flying boat as an air gunner and was sent to West Africa."

"In June 1941 I was accepted into the Women's Land Army. I was told that 250 girls were being sent to Kent to help harvest up and to spend six months working on the threshing machine. As I left that day I wondered what I had let myself in for – I didn't even know what a threshing machine was, let alone what we would be harvesting! My orders soon came through telling me to report to Midland Station at Bedford by 10.00am on 5 August to catch a train to St Pancras. Thankfully a friend I had made while working in Greens was also being sent to Kent. Her name was Joan Davey and was I pleased to see someone I knew. We boarded the train and as we set off we were informed we were going to Romney Marsh. As it was a place neither Joan or I had ever head of, we wondered just what it would be like. Many of us imagined being stuck out alone on wet marsh lands. When we got to St Pancras Station we had to make our way to London Bridge. The sight that met our eyes I shall never forget. Just hundreds and hundreds of girls all dressed the same in green jumpers and fawn riding breaches. We were given a talk and told how much the war effort now depended on our efforts and that the work we would be doing would be so vital for the future of our homeland. We were then marched off to get the train that was to take us to Kent. The train stopped at quite a few stations and girls left the train. We watched as they grouped up to march off to start their new lives. Then at last we reached Ashford where we departed the train. I think more got off here than anywhere else. Once outside the station a whole line of cars and vans etc. were waiting for us. I myself had not ridden in a car for at least 10 years and was looking forward to it once again. There were four of us in our car: Ruby, Joan, Betty and myself."

"We were driven to New Romney where we were billeted with a Mrs Bingham. We could see at once what a lovely lady she was and she soon made us all feel at home. We were told that until we were needed to work the threshing machine, we were to start work for a Mr Gorden on his farm at Old Romney. So next morning we all reported to him. Of course we had no transport so we had to walk everywhere. To get to Old Romney we went across the fields. Poor Mr Gorden – he was so very patient with us girls, for none of us knew anything about farming and needless to say, for quite a while we made a mess of most of the tasks we were given to do. Most mornings when we crossed the fields for work, we came out into a lane that took us into Old Romney and every morning we met a herd of cows which were just returning to the fields after being milked. We always waited until they had gone by before we entered the lane and walked behind the herdsman. We always walked well behind them for we were afraid of them, especially the big bull that walked by the herdsman. How I remember one certain morning when I said to the herdsman 'would that bull charge and hurt us if we were to walk in front of it?' He just burst out laughing and tears were rolling down his face. He just couldn't stop. Us girls thought he must be mad, and we looked at one another wondering to ourselves whether *he* was safe, let alone the bull. Once he managed to stop laughing he said 'you city girls have got a lot to learn. This 'ere ain't a bull, it's my family Jersey cow. She won't hurt you at all, but you better soon learn to tell a bull from a cow or else you'll be in trouble'. What fools we girls felt, but all the other cows looked so different from this one that we just assumed it was a bull!"

"By next morning I think the whole village knew what a bright bunch of girls we were, but to be fair they never made a big thing out of it, for I believe they knew we were willing to learn and were doing our best."

"Our work at this time started at 7.30am and we finished at 5.00pm. If there was no extra work to be done Mrs Bingham got us up at 6.00am and always had a big cooked breakfast for us. While we sat and ate it she made our sandwiches for the day. When we returned in the evening there was always a wonderful home cooked meal for us and a nice steamed pudding for sweet. All this she cooked on an old black range which she fuelled with whatever she could to keep the fire going so that she could prepare such wonderful meals. We had no gas or electricity, only oil lamps, so the old cooking range was so very important for us. As well as cooking on it, Mrs Bingham boiled all our hot water on it, and of course it provided heat in the winter months."

"We were so very lucky that we had been sent to work on Mr Gordan Finn-Kelcey's Farm for he was a real gentleman and he never once lost his temper with any of us girls. When I think what he had to put up with from us all I can see what a miracle it was, and I thank God that he also had the patience of a saint." (At the time of writing Marion's story, Mr Finn-Kelcey is 92).

"During June and July, while I had been working at the shop in Bedford, the weather had been lovely and I had envied all those Land Army girls who came in looking so tanned and well looking. This was one of the reasons I joined the Land Army. Well, sure enough, when August arrived I think the weather had seen me coming, for it was so very wet and we all looked such a sorry sight in our horrible green macs. For the whole of August we had to wear them in our attempts to keep dry. The job we were given to do at this time was thistle picking and every time we thought that it was all done, we were taken to another field of crops for more of the same. We were so pleased when one day it was raining so hard, we were given the job of clearing out the old farm outbuildings. We also mended the sacks ready to put produce in. We did not mind this at all – at least we were out of the rain. I can assure you it was no fun working wet through all day. Mrs Bingham was so very good to us and when we arrived back each night at her house she would have gallons of boiling water ready for us girls to bathe in. Those old tin baths were a godsend after a hard days work; it was just heaven to relax and soak in them."

"September came and better weather was with us. We cut a field of turnip seed and laid it out in rows to dry out. I think as long as I live I will never forget the day we started threshing it. We had a sledge that was about the same as a large trailer but it was very low to the ground and was drawn by one of the lovely old shire horses. They certainly were gentle giants and of course they reminded me of my childhood days when I would feed the milkman and coalman's horses. We had to lay a very large canvas sheet on the floor of the trailer then we loaded on the bundles of turnip seed and the stalks. Two of us girls then had to tread it all down to flatten it out so that we could get as much onto the trailer as possible – our poor legs would get scratched to bits. We then took it to the threshing machine, where the seed was separated from the straw etc. Then we would bag up the seed and load it onto another trailer. Even though these sacks were very heavy, before long us girls were lifting them as well as the men were. I think I must point out that when I arrived at Mrs Bingham's I weighed in at 8st 4lbs, but after a while I was up to 10st 7lbs all thanks to Mrs Bingham's wonderful cooking and plenty of fresh air to give you a hearty appetite."

"One lovely hot day when we were threshing the turnip seed, we worked on late into the evening and there was a real harvest moon. We thought at the time how romantic it was threshing by moonlight. This was soon forgotten once we finished for the day, for we still had our long walk back to Mrs Bingham's across the fields. We were all dead on our feet and by now it was quite dark, and of course Mrs Bingham had no idea where we were as we had no 'phones in those days to let her know that we would be late. She soon got used to it though, and on such nights when we were late and it was dark, as long as there was no air raid on, she would leave the curtain to the front room window open a little and stand an oil lamp in it. This light would guide us home across the fields. It didn't matter what time we arrived back – she always had hot water for us and, of course, a hot meal. She really was as good as any mother to us girls and if ever one of us was out at night she would wait up until we arrived home so that she knew we were safe – it didn't matter what time it was. And she would still be up in the morning to call us girls, and prepare one of her lovely cooked breakfasts for us which set us up for the day."

"We spent seven weeks with Mr Finn-Kelcey then we were told the threshing machine we were to use was ready and that the workload would take us through until the next April. We soon became known around the area as the threshing girls. Mr Finn-Kelcey told us how sad he was that we were leaving his workforce and asked Ruby and I whether, once the threshing season had finished, we would come back to work for him and help him with the planting."

"By now us girls were getting to know most of the people in New Romney and the surrounding area. In New Romney there were many Newfoundland soldiers who were training etc. They always took the mickey out of us Land Army girls and our uniforms, and would call out to us "ride 'em cowboys" whenever they saw us on our bikes, which we had been issued with to help us get around much faster. Every Saturday evening we would attend the local dance at The Ship public house, which was always so overcrowded that you could hardly move, let alone dance. Some Saturdays Mrs Bingham would come with us and it would be so nice to see her enjoying herself for she worked so hard all week to make us girls feel happy. Deep down I think she knew we all missed our homes and families. She really was a wonderful lady and on these Saturday evenings she joined in the singing and dancing just as if she was one of the girls."

"We also had so many army regiments nearby that we got to meet a lot of soldiers at these dances. I remember the Yorkshire regiment being near to us, which made me feel at home when I chatted to them about where I lived in Yorkshire as a child. We also had the Royal Irish Guards regiment with us for a short time. They looked so smart in their orange kilts and they had a good band with a lovely Irish wolfhound that walked at the front."

"Ruby and I went to Hythe church for their farewell service before they went off to fight abroad. It was a service I will always remember – it was so very moving. I have often wondered how many of the lads came through it all and were able to come home and have a life after doing their part for King and country. We also had the Royal Engineers near to us, who were running the light railway for the area. They would take us to dances at the Turnpike Camp. All of these soldiers were perfect gentlemen and made us girls feel so very special. On one occasion we were coming back from one of these dances on the train when the sirens had sounded. It was a hot summer's evening and everywhere was so dry. We thought we had stopped because of the threat of an air raid but we soon found out that sparks from the engine had set light to the grass on the side of the track and was starting to get near to the fields of crops. All of these wonderful soldiers got out of the train took off their army tunics and began beating at the flames, for of course it was lighting up the train and surrounding area and would be a welcome light to enemy aircraft. The lads soon had the fire under control and managed to save it from reaching the crops, but alas their tunics were ruined. The whole area was so proud of them, and I am sure their Commanding Officer saw to it that they received new tunics, and of course were thanked for what they had done."

"One day soon after this, Mrs Bingham told us four girls that she had some bad news for us. We all feared something really terrible but she told us that her son, who was in the R.A.F., had made her an allowance, and this, together with the money she received for looking after us girls, would affect her widows pension, so from now on she could only keep two of us with her. Ruby and I were the lucky ones that were to stay. Betty and Joan were billeted in Station Road, which was not far from us but however good it was for them there, I know they missed Mrs Bingham and the way she had mothered them."

"The work was very hard now with so much to be done, and one day we were given the job of repairing a haystack. We had to climb to the top of it to remove the thatch. There were plenty of screams from us girls, for as soon as we started removing it, mice and rats jumped out at us which frightened us no end. When we had removed it all and had come down to earth again, Mr John Homewood who was our boss at this time, asked us what job we would like to do instead. I said I would like to be on the threshing machine and my request was granted. Later that day whilst working on the threshing machine, which was some distance from the stack, we saw an aeroplane come over with its engine trailing out smoke. Someone shouted 'he's in trouble, he's going to crash'. They also said 'it's not one of ours, it's a German plane. I bet he's on his way back from a raid on London'. He went low over the haystack and out of sight. Someone said 'I bet he's managed to land in one of the fields'. We all grabbed our pitchforks and set off to get him. As we neared the haystack a chap came round the side of it shouting in a foreign language. One of the girls said 'he must be the German pilot' so we shouted to him 'put your hands up' and held our pitch forks out at him, then marched him off to the village bobby. When we got him there did we have egg on our faces – we had only arrested a German prisoner of war who was working in a nearby field and had come running to get help as he had seen a plane come down. What the outcome was I can't remember – we felt so silly for what we had done, we dare not ask any questions for fear of having people laugh at us."

"Our threshing team consisted of 14, made up of us four girls, young school leavers, old age pensioners and farm labourers. We took it in turns to do the different jobs such as cutting strings as the shooks went into the thresher – this is a job I liked doing best of all. You had to cut the string where the knot was and, of course, all the string had to be saved. The straw that came away from the machine had to be baled and stacked ready to use as straw in the farm sheds and yard etc. Two men stood at the rear of the machine where bags were hooked onto special hooks to catch the seed. These bags weighed 2cwt and, as I have said before, although some farmers thought we should be able to unhook the bags and carry them when full to put them onto the scales, most thought that it was just too much for us girls to do, so we were grateful that these men would not let us try to lift them."

"Our hours of work at this time were 7.30am start and we finished at 9.30pm. We did have a one hour lunchbreak and 15 minutes in the afternoon for a cup of tea. When finished we would cycle back to Mrs Bingham's and oh, how good that hot bath would feel on our aching limbs. As we took our clothes off there would be chaff and dust everywhere; the seed got into your underwear, your socks – you name it, it was there. Looking back, it really was a filthy job but someone had to do it, and I think it really was a miracle that we were able to have a nice hot bath when finished, all thanks to dear Mrs Bingham."

"When I look back I can see that they were some of the hardest days of my life, but it really did teach me to stand on my own two feet. My wages at the time were 2 pounds 2 shillings a week. I paid 22 shillings a week for my board, and out of the £1.00 I had left I would buy my soap, toothpaste, shoe polish etc. Of course, all my washing was done by hand, as there were no washing machines in those days, and if we had clothes which were really dirty then we boiled them on the old cooking range in one of Mrs Bingham's old saucepans. The rest of my money I would save towards my Saturday nights out and for my trips home to see my mother."

"One of the best farms I worked on was that of Mr Boyd at St Mary in the Marsh, for not only did I meet my darling John here, who was to become a wonderful husband to me, and father of my lovely children, but also my memory of working on Mr Boyd's farm is one of great happiness, for here we were always given hot drinks and wonderful buns to eat – a thing all of us girls really did appreciate."

"Here I was also to meet two wonderful old characters – Jack and Bill Lancaster. They always made us laugh with their stories which made the day go by so quickly. I also remember the kindness of Mr and Mrs Carey at Warren Farm, New Romney and how Mrs Carey would take us into her kitchen when it was cold and make us one of her wonderful hot chocolate drinks and allow us to get warmed through, for I think the winter of 1941 was one of the worst for the people of the marsh. We couldn't ride our bikes for ages, owing to the ice on the roads. This pleased Ruby, for until she received her bike from the Land Army she had never been on one in her life. She was always falling off, and cut herself quite badly at times, but she always said "I'll get the hang of the damn thing if it kills me". Thankfully it never killed her, but when the roads were covered with ice we, like her, were only too pleased to leave our bikes at Mrs Bingham's and walk everywhere once again. To reach all the farms that we worked on at this time, we used to walk on the nice even surfaces of the frozen ditches, as all of the fields had all been ploughed. Today the fields don't seem to have so many hedgerows and ditches which is a shame really as they provided a home for so many birds and animals."

"Sometimes the roads were so bad that they couldn't move the threshing machine onto another farm and so instead of three days at a farm we would stay and do whatever we could until the roads got better.

Our first Christmas came and we were going home for a week to tell everyone of our war effort and the part we were playing in keeping our country going. Ruby and I asked one of the men if he could get us a goose and a rabbit to take home with us for Christmas. Imagine our surprise when he turned up early on the morning of our departure just as we were leaving to catch the train at 7.00am, with two geese still with all their feathers on and four rabbits still with all their fur. Did we have a laugh on the train as it began to fill up with soldiers. The train stopped at so many stations (I think it stopped at eight before we even reached Ashford), and even in that short time we could have sold our fare many times over. When we arrived at London and changed trains we walked over London Bridge with the geese and rabbits thrown over our shoulders as they were so heavy. Their blood dripped all down the back of us, but it wasn't until later that we realised this, when we found the backs of our stockings covered in it. The worst job was still to come, for once we arrived home at Bedford the geese had to be plucked and the rabbits had to be skinned. You just try plucking a goose that's stone cold – no wonder I have never had a goose since that Christmas of 1941."

"We had a marvellous Christmas – by now my mum had taken in four evacuee children, and their sets of parents had come to be with them for Christmas as well, except for some of their fathers who were away fighting the enemy. We all mucked in, as everyone did in those days, and it turned out to be such a wonderful Christmas for us all. Of course I went to Mill Street Baptist Church, where I had spent so many happy hours before I went into the Land Army. I found now, though, that each time I went, there were fewer of the people I knew, as so many of them had gone off to war to fight for our homeland. The week soon passed and it was back to Kent and back to work."

"The country was still in the grips of winter so we were kept busy on the threshing machine with beans, peas for linseed plus barley and oats. We spent the cold winter nights huddled together in front of the range at Mrs Bingham's house and she was so very good in letting us bring our friends home. Sometimes the old characters would come and sit and tell us their tales of life in the 1860s – such wonderful stories they would tell of how life was when they were growing up – talk about Oliver Twist. They really were such moving stories and even though we were in the grips of war, it made us girls feel lucky to be living in such times."

"Mrs Bingham would even bake potatoes, wrap them in silver paper and take them to the soldiers on guard duty at 10.00pm every night for, as she said, "these dear boys are guarding our lanes and byeways and will need food and drink to keep them going". Of course many of these lads, when not on duty, would visit us all at Mrs Bingham's and sit and play cards with us and just chat about our past lives and of our families, for whatever situation you are in it is always a help to speak of your loved ones. As you know, for so many of our dear boys who were prisoners of the Japanese and Germans, it was the thoughts of their loved ones back home that kept them going, even when death was staring them in the face."

"I believe at this time my father was working in Baghdad after his nightmare of getting out of Poland. I think it came as a shock to my mother when he went abroad again to work. Now that I am old myself, looking back I don't know how she carried on all alone, especially with all us children gone, for by now young Olive Mai had also joined the Land Army and went to work on a farm in the Bedford area. This meant that all three of us girls were now Land Army girls and I know mum was very proud of this; and she was just as proud of our brother Billy for the part he was playing in the war when he could have stayed in his reserved occupation. I can remember as if it were yesterday, the last leave Billy had before he went to Freetown, West Africa..... Mrs Bingham allowed him to come and stay with us and I managed to get a few days off. We really did enjoy ourselves together. We always were so very close as Billy was only 13 months older than me. I showed him around the area and took him to the dances and was so very proud to be able to show him off to all the girls. I would like to think he really enjoyed his stay with me before he went off to war again, for it was to be the last time we would ever see one another, for my dear Billy died on a mission. My mother received a letter telling her that Billy was missing, believed killed in action. I know the bottom of her world dropped out at that time for although I know she loved us girls she had often told us that she wished she'd had four boys for they were nowhere near as much trouble as girls!"

"Mr Finn-Kelcey and everyone else around me at that time was so very good to me. They wanted me to go home to grieve and to be with my mother but I knew it would do Billy no good now and I knew that my father was home and I believed he and mother needed time to be together and share their sad loss. I knew that Olive Mai would be near to them as well, as she was on a farm near to R.A.F. Henlow, and Betty was at Kempston Home for orphans, so I knew they would be there for mum and dad if they wanted them."

"Christmas 1942 came and by now I had met my John who worked on the farms. I knew I had fallen in love with him and wanted to be with him as much as I could. I asked him to come home with me for the holidays and so we went home to Bedford together for Christmas with my family. I think that even though Bedford had so many R.A.F. stations in the area it is fair to say we did not get bombed too much. I remember that at least we were able to get out and about by walking. Where Betty was working, they put on a Christmas party and she asked us to go along. It was a good three miles from our house and we walked all the way there and back. It was a wonderful party put on by the Matron, Miss Carter, and although food was on ration and things were hard, the American airmen and our Air Force boys helped with the food and drink, which was a wonderful thing to do, not just for the party but for the care of those dear children who had lost their mums and dads. It really brought home to me the hurt of war, and the suffering it causes for us ordinary families."

"We walked home after midnight. It really was a lovely moonlit night and I gave thanks to God for my being so very lucky to have my John with me, and not in some foreign land fighting or being held as a prisoner of war. He had tried to join up on many occasions, but his poor health always let him down, so he was sent to work on the farms to get plenty of fresh air. I thank God that he was, for I know how lucky I was to meet him and fall in love with him. We had planned to marry on 20th March, and how lucky we were to have Betty in Bedford, for she really did arrange everything for us, even as far as getting the wedding cake made for us and it was all iced as well – a miracle in war time!"

"My friend Ruby's sister had been married in 1942 and she offered to lend me her wedding dress. This was a godsend as even in the Land Army we had to use our clothing coupons to buy all our clothes to work in. So I was pleased to borrow it, along with two bridesmaids dresses for Betty and Ruby. Olive Mai had borrowed a dress from one of her friends so I think the bit about having something borrowed was well and truly covered. My something new was my wedding ring which cost 25 shillings, but to me it is priceless. My something blue was easy to sort out by wearing something blue. The something old was my shoes, for the only ones I had were my Land Army shoes and of course I couldn't wear these with a wedding dress so one of the family lent me an old pair of shoes, for which I was very grateful – they looked much smarter than my boots!"

"The great day soon arrived – 20th March 1943. The ceremony was held at Mill Street Baptist Church. It was a small gathering of just family really, as we just couldn't afford much at that time. John's mum and dad came, and his sister Agnes, but his brother Jim was away fighting the Germans in the deserts of Africa, working in the tanks trying to stop Rommel. Of course my mum and dad were there, Betty and Olive Mai, and my aunt Rea who (along with her dear sister who had died from breast cancer at such a young age) had made all the wonderful dresses for the well-to-do ladies. She had never married, but cared for my grandparents until they died well into their 80's."

"It was a very happy day but I think it hit us all that our dear Billy was not with us, having made the ultimate sacrifice for his King and country. After the wedding reception John and I caught the train to Hitchin where we stayed at the Sun Hotel. Many people may say 'what a place to stay for your honeymoon' but it was war time and that was all that we could afford for a few days, and well, does it really matter where you spend your honeymoon as long as you are together? Most of the other guests at the hotel were old people but they were very kind to John and I, and all wished us well in our life together."

"Before we knew it Saturday came and we were back at Romney Marsh. John was working for Mr Boyd and he had to be at work on the Sunday morning by 6.30am to milk the cows, and so ended our first and last week's holiday for many a year to come. In time I got my release from the Land Army as long as I agreed to keep working on the land, so I went to work for Mr Boyd along with John and I think it fair to say that after a while I could do all the jobs that they did, as well as driving the tractors and trailers. John and I also had to find somewhere to live, and as all the houses had been comandeered by the army, this was an impossible task, so John's mother and father asked us to move in with them at their house, Gable Lodge. I didn't think much to it to be honest, but at least it meant that John and I could be together. I soon realised how much I had been spoilt at Mrs Bingham's for I soon found out that being married was to be hard work. I would start work at 8.00am and would make our packed lunch for us, sandwiches of course, and John and I would have our lunch break together. I would finish at 5.00pm and once home would prepare and cook the evening meal ready for us all to eat at 7.00pm, then after clearing away and washing up it was around 9.00pm before we got to sit down and of course after a day in the fresh air and a good meal, you soon fell asleep. In the summer months the hours were much different. From June until September we were lucky to finish work by 9.00pm and, in October, with the harvest all finished, we started on potatoes which meant more hard work."

"Mr Boyd employed around 16 men in all, working with the cows and on the land. It really was a lovely farm to work on and everyone got on so well, especially the older men who always had wonderful tales of the old days to tell us. So you see nothing has changed, for now that I am old I am passing on my own story so that the next generation will know what it was like for me in my lifetime."

"Another job I had to do along with the men was the muck

spreading, for which at times you really did need to wear a clothes peg on your nose, such was the smell. You can imagine the jokes and comments that were made. There was always plenty of muck as Mr Boyd had a dairy herd, and it was a job that had to be done, for in those days there were no fertilizers like there are available today, so all we had for the land was good old muck and natural fertilizer!"

"As John and I now had farming in our blood we tried to rent or buy a piece of land to try and farm ourselves, but of course we couldn't compete with the big farmers who soon snapped up any land that came up for sale. So when John's father retired in 1943, he said he would come in with us and would sell Gable Lodge, so he instructed John to find a farm where we could all work and live together. The farm John found for us was in Colchester in Essex – it had a large house and 30 acres of land, so this meant we had to leave Kent, which I know was a sad day for all of us."

"John and I went first to get things sorted out and ready for his parents to join us some three months later. It really was so good to have John all to myself and for the first time in our married life we were really alone at last together. It was very hard work for us getting the place straight and after working on the land all day, at night we tried to get the house around to how we wanted it. The couple who had farmed the farm before us, a Mr and Mrs Charlie Simpson, had now retired and lived in a cottage next to us. They were so very helpful and Charlie even helped John on the farm with all the manual work. We only had an old tractor, a binder and plough – no car, not even a telephone – so all our travelling was done by bike. At this time I kept being sick, and John and I wondered if I had something wrong with me, so to keep him happy I went to see the doctor. After he examined me he said 'nothing to worry about Mrs Andrews, you're just pregnant. You just carry on as usual, nature will take its course all in good time'. People often say 'new house, new baby' and this was certainly true for me. John's mother and father came to join us in May 1944, which kept us busy for it meant two more to cook for. The only toilet we had was an old wooden hut at the bottom of the garden, with an old bucket, which reminded me of my school days. I told John how the school caretaker had done very well with his produce from his garden with the help of the bucket's contents. I don't think he thought much to it though – he always dug a large hole and buried the contents of ours!"

"As I was having the baby at home, like everyone did in those days, my mum was coming to look after me. When she arrived at the station, which was a good three miles away, she was in for a nice surprise. Charlie had borrowed a pony and trap and had gone to meet her. Remember, the only transport we had ourselves was our bikes. It was a real treat for mum, and I believe she thought she was back in Ireland for she had grown up riding in pony and traps. Since we had moved to Essex we had seen much more of our air force as there were so many airfields around the area, and before long we would be counting the planes out when they went off on a mission, and counting them back in hours later. You won't need me to tell you how many dear boys lost their lives up in the skies protecting our homeland."

"Early in the morning of June 6th I woke up wanting to go to the loo but I had the feeling that I kept wanting to go. Mum started to panic in case I had the baby in the bucket. She said to John 'get your bike out and go and get the nurse' which meant a three mile ride for John and off he went, half awake. Outside everything was going mad, there were planes going over in their droves so we knew that Germany was in for it.... or were they our planes coming back? In the panic we couldn't tell if they were coming or going, but there really was a lot of them. The nurse arrived about one hour later and began getting me ready. Mum was busy boiling water up on our Calor gas cooker and our old solid fuel stove. I think she boiled up so much we would have had enough to bath the whole village in but at least it kept her occupied. At 10.00am John was told once again to get his bike out and to go for the doctor. I think I was alright though, and looking back I had an easy birth so perhaps the nurse just wanted him out of the way."

"At 10.45am I gave birth to my darling baby girl Jean Margaret, who weighed in at 8lb 12oz. As Mrs Simpson put it when she first saw her 'what a lovely little mite she is'. Yes, the 6th of June 1944 had not only brought D-Day but also my lovely baby. We soon realised why all the planes had been so very busy once we knew that it was D-Day."

"My mum stayed with me for two weeks but she and my mother-in-law were poles apart and three women in one house was a nightmare, so after two weeks I managed on my own. John and I were so very happy, as you can imagine, and we were starting to make many friends and beginning to feel settled. Jean was so very good and soon came to work with us and would sit in her pram and watch us working. It was hard work, of course, but we so much wanted to make a go of it. Then one day John's mother said she was not happy and would have to move back to Romney Marsh, so she and John's dad would have to sell the farm. We had no real say in it as it was their money that had bought the farm anyway. The farm was sold and we all went back to Kent. Jean was now about 15 months old and, thank God, John was able to get his job back with Mr Boyd on his farm. After the sale of the farm John and I received £900 as our share of what we had put into it. With the money we bought 2 Seabourne Way and John's mum and dad rented a flat in Folkstone. Once again it was to be 'new home, new baby' for I was now expecting again. It was now 1945, the year that was to bring the end of World War II and when VJ Day came on 15th August it was one of the happiest days of everyone's lives, for all the hard work we had put into the war effort had paid off. I think when we saw those dear boys who arrived home in October after being prisoners of the Japanese, we couldn't believe our eyes. They were like walking skeletons, and I think it fair to say it is only in the last few years, now that it has started to be talked about, that we at last have learned what they really gave and suffered for us all to have a life today."

"John was working very hard and long hours now, and we managed to save just a little and were able to buy a small car. What a luxury it was after biking everywhere. It even meant that John was able to come home at midday for lunch; it was so nice for us to have this hour break together for throughout the war we had shared our lunch-breaks together and thanks to our little car he soon arrived home, for in those days the roads in the area had nowhere near as many cars on them as they have today."

"Everyone in England was now working hard to get our country back on to its feet, and this really was the case for us who worked on the land. The great feeling of comradeship that had helped us through the war years was still with us, for I don't think there were many families that had not been scared by the war in some way, most of them having lost a son or husband, or in many cases even a wife and mother. In my case it was my dear brother Billy and to this day I treasure my memories of our childhood days together as we played in the fields and meadows of dear old Yorkshire."

"February 1946 came and this was to be the month for the birth of my second child. My mother came down to be with me again and thank God she did, for John had gone off to work and all through the night I had been getting pains, but thought it was nothing to worry about. But by 10.00am I was getting such bad pains at regular intervals that I knew the little one was ready to come into the world. Mum asked the man next door if he would go to Dymchurch to get the doctor, which he did. But I couldn't wait for the doctor to arrive, and at 11.45am I gave birth to my son Richard. As the doctor was not there my mum did all the necessary and delivered him for me. When John got home for lunch at 12.00 noon mum met him at the door and said 'come you on young man, you have a son'. Poor John couldn't relax though, and because as no doctor or nurse had been he was sent off to find one of them. He found the nurse who was busy delivering another baby. She came as quickly as she could but when she did arrive the doctor had already got to me. He praised mum for her sterling work which really pleased her. He weighed Richard who weighed in at 9lbs and told us what a fine baby he was. The date of this wonderful day in my life was 20th February – another day I will never forget."

"We knew now that we were a real family and I think that the days from 1946 until 1948 were the laziest of my life, for even though they say it's hard work bringing up children, it was nowhere near as hard as my war years working on the land. We had two very hot summers in those two years, and did I enjoy myself with the children and my friends around the village who also had young children. Most days we would walk to the beach and sit and chat while the children played together – such wonderful days."

"In 1949 we were given the chance of renting our own farm. Friends of John's mother and father owned Great Lathe Farm, which they rented out during the war years but it had become run down. As they were getting too old to work the farm now, and it was upsetting them to see it in such a state, they asked John if he would like to rent it and work it for himself. Of course it was something that John and I had always wanted to do – to have our own farm was always our dream. So we decided to go for it. We sold our house in Seabourne Way and with the money we bought machinery and the things we would need. I was expecting again but we didn't mind for we were still so in love and were really looking forward to our new baby. So in March 1949 we moved into Great Lathe. The old house was in a terrible state as the army had used it during the war, and it really was in bad repair. I feel sure the army must have paid compensation for the condition it was in but we could see none of it had been spent on the house and so John and I found ourselves with a lot of work on our hands again. The farm itself had around 80 acres and a very large house with, downstairs, a large kitchen, plus three large rooms, and the big cold dairy room. Upstairs we had three big bedrooms plus a large store room, and in the attic two more cold rooms. This was now to be home for us."

"We took over the livestock with the farm and I remember we had around 60 sheep which were terribly neglected, and as they were due to lamb in April, it was really hard work for us. We lost 18 of them and thought to ourselves 'what a beginning', but once the sheep were better looked after, things really improved."

"I was still riding my bike around. I would have Jean in a seat on the back and little Richard on a front seat. A friend of mine, Annie Rayner, said to me many years later 'we in the village always felt sorry for you at the time, having to ride around on your bike with two and a half children with you', for my new baby was due in May, around the 21st, I was told. However, he couldn't wait, and arrived on the 14th May 1949. We named him Stephen William. He arrived into the world at 1.00pm on that day weighing 9lbs. Jean started school that September, so I was soon left with two to care for during the day. I would help John all I could as we still couldn't afford to employ anyone and John would say 'come on love, it's time to put that women's Land Army training into practice' and I would find myself hoeing up all the weeds. I didn't mind though, and in time we did employ someone to help us with our growing of wurzel, sugar beet, corn, peas and beans. At harvest time it was all hands to the pump, so to speak, and all manner of people would come and help us, working well into the night if the weather was good. We really had to make hay while the sun shined."

"One of the jobs I have always loved was the building of the hay stacks – when they were finished you really could stand back and admire your work. We thatched the tops of the stacks with reeds from the ditches and some of the men really did create masterpieces – a real sight to behold. Stacking the peas was such a dirty job – they were always so dusty, and seed etc. would be all over you, but they had to be left stacked until the threshing machine came round which could be up to six months later. Of course it was something I always loved to see and after all the time I had spent on them in the war, it was always a pleasure to work on them again."

"When it came to doing the sugar beet, it was always so cold and your hands would often be frost-bitten. Once the beet was lifted it had to be topped and tailed and loaded into a heap ready for collection. It really was back-breaking work. We also had to notify New Romney Station and the beet factory that we had a load coming. So on the day before, we would spend the day loading the beet onto trailers then at 7.00am the next morning John would go off in the tractor and trailer with the sugar beet and I would follow on in the car with the children. It meant that they had to have an early breakfast on these days and after I had helped John unload the beet onto the station wagon, it was time to take them to school in Dymchurch, that is once they had all started school. I would then rush back to the farm and help with loading the beet onto the trailer again then John and I would be backwards and forwards to the station until we had loaded all our beet into the wagons for delivery to the beet factory. Of course in the meantime I now had our cows, pigs, sheep and chickens to feed and check on, and I always had David, our faithful dog, with us. We had him when Jean was just three weeks old and I don't think Jean could have had a better nursemaid for he would sit by her pram all the time and watch over her."

"After a few years we began to really get results from the farm, after all our hard work that we had put in. One day, Mr Boyd, who was not really one to give praise, for he too was used to hard work, called to see us and he said 'John, I never thought you would be able to pull this place round. You have turned it from a grade 3 farm into a grade 1 farm'. We knew that after someone like Mr Boyd had said this, we really had what it takes to be farmers, and I think we worked even harder then to make sure this was the case. As the children were growing, they too helped us, and soon we were growing potatoes as well. We also had a strawberry patch and in time we sold produce from the back door. I used to take our eggs round door-to-door as well, and soon had a regular weekly round. I loved meeting all the people and it enabled me to make many more friends."

"With all the hard work the years soon flew by, and in time we bought Great Lathe Farm, a thing we were so very proud of. We always knew we were not going to be given anything on a plate, and the only way we were going to get on was by hard work, and when I think back of how dear John was with his health problems, it really was a miracle how well he had done for us. In 1954 my father-in-law was taken ill and had to go into Canterbury Hospital for treatment. It was very hard for John at this time for after working all day on the farm he would take his mother to visit his father. When his father died, his mother couldn't cope on her own and for a while John stayed with her at night, but she was in such a state I suggested that she come and live with us. With my three children and her it was like having four children to care for. She made the most work though, for in time I had to wash and do everything for her. Our youngest child, Stephen, had not yet started school and I think he suffered the most, for I fear he was always pushed to one side while I cared for his gran. He was a great little fellow though, and would help me with the chickens and animals and do all he could for his gran."

"In 1957 John's mother died and after a while things went back to normal, if life on a farm can ever be called normal that is. In 1959 my own mother fell ill. She came to live with us for the last few months of her life. She was no trouble at all, and after all she had done for me in my life it was my privilege to care for her until the end."

"Also in 1959, I went as a delegate to the Albert Hall in London on behalf of the Burmarsh Village Women's Institute, which we formed in 1950. I really did enjoy these monthly meetings, for it was the only time I ever left the farm and got out of the house on my own. I don't want to sound ungrateful, but I think just to have a little time on my own did me good and if anything made me an even better mother. As I was to be away for two days, Margot, my sister-in-law asked me to stay with her, for which I was grateful. My children now were growing fast – Jean was now 15, Richard was 13 and Stephen was 10. So John could manage more on his own now and I know the children were a great help to him as well. It was June and it was getting near to our busy time so those couple of days away gave me a nice break, but once back to the farm it was all hands to the pump for there was plenty of hard work to do. The harvest time came which meant many late nights for, as all farmers know, it's very long days for all involved at harvest time. We had no modern combine harvesters in those days, the only thing we had was our hands and some very early farm machinery, so it really was as the saying goes.... many hands make light work."

"In September I was feeling ill again but just thought I had overdone it at harvest time. John said 'you get along to the doctor' and I said 'look what happened the last time you sent me to the doctors!' He replied 'you get along there and find out then'. Well, the doctor confirmed what I thought.... yes, I was pregnant again. My friends joked with me, 'that's what happens when you leave the marsh and go gallivanting off to London'. Even the people on my egg round who knew I had been to the Albert Hall started to refer to my unborn child as Albert. When I visited them each week with their eggs they would say 'and how is young Albert getting on? I hope he's not kicking out at you too much.' They all used to worry about me and tell me to take things easy for a while, but things had not changed that much since the war, for there was always plenty of hard work to do and you couldn't tell farm animals that you were going to have a break for too long as they always needed feeding and milking etc. I must admit, though, that the children were so very good and helped John and I all they could. I must also admit that there were days when the work was so hard and long that I used to think back to how lucky I was when working in the shops when I was a young girl, but I didn't dwell on it for long as the land was now my life and John and I had come so far along life's road together. And, of all things, we had the war to thank for bringing us together, and now here we were with 1960 coming along and we were to have our fourth child.... oh how lucky we were."

"The nurse started to call on me a couple of times a week now to examine me, and just after Christmas she was very worried about my blood pressure and my heart. I was sent to Folkestone Hospital to see a specialist to see if I was to have to go into hospital to have the baby. He said I could go home and, as long as I took things easy, that he could not see why I shouldn't have my baby at home just as I had done with my other children. As he said this I was so very happy for it was what I wanted – the only sad thing for me was that my dear mother would not be with me this time. I went home and made sure I had everything prepared, then a month later on my birthday, I started getting the pains that all mothers will know about. We now had a telephone so we called for the nurse who came at midnight as I was well into labour. So, on 15th April at 7.00am my new baby arrived weighing in at 10lb 8ozs. My boys went out as soon as she was born for they had put up a large flag pole in one of the fields, where they

41

raised a union jack to let the villagers know that the baby had arrived. It was Good Friday, so most people had the day off and word soon spread that our baby had been born. We called her Julie and we were all so pleased to have her safely with us in our family. The nurse asked Jean if she would help get everything ready for her visits and if she would help bath her. To this day I think it helped make up Jean's mind that she too would become a nurse. The only thing Jean did not want to do was take the baby out for a walk in the pram on her own for fear that people would think the baby was hers. It was very hard work starting to care for a baby again and I was so thankful to all my other children as they were all very good with little Julie. Richard was so good with her and would do anything for her, which of course was a great help to me. They were all such wonderful children and we all worked together on the farm – the boys would do most things with John, and Jean was not far behind them. Little Julie would sit in her pushchair and watch us and when she got bored one of us would always take a break and play with her, for such is the life of a working farming family."

We shall leave Marion's story here for the stories of her children's lives are their business but I know they have all worked hard, just like mum and dad, and have all done well in their chosen careers, which I know Marion and John were both very proud of. I say were both very proud, for sadly in 1993 dear John was taken from our planet earth to take his place in paradise. That day, 26th March, was the day that Marion lost the love of her life.

Today, Great Lathe Farm is run by her son Richard and his wife, but Marion is still there helping out and doing her bit and as I said at the very beginning of her story, she can be found in Gran's Shop, which is now her second home. She loves meeting and speaking with people, and I would urge you all to visit her down on the farm and take a look around the wonderful museum which really is a tribute to her John and to all the Land Army girls and farm workers who did so much to keep our country alive in World War II. After your look round I dare say you will be ready for a drink and something to eat, and I can think of nowhere better than Great Lathe Tea Rooms where you can sit and discuss all that you have seen in the museum and farm.

Yes, when World War II came you can see it really did change

Marion's life. Even if it has been a life of hard work, it has been a full and interesting one. Little could she have imagined when she went off from Bedford Station that morning on 5th August 1941 that from that day onwards the land would be her life. Having met Marion and able to count her among my friends, I also know what a great missionary or childrens' nurse she would have made, but this was not to be and like so many other Land Army girls the land became her life and still is to this day. She really is one great lady and I feel sure the people of Burmarsh know just how lucky they are to have her among them and, who knows, perhaps by sharing her story with us here she has really helped put Burmarsh on the map for it really has played a big part in her wonderful life.

You may like to know that Marion's father did finish his days of working abroad and came home to spend many happy years with Olive at Bedford where they also enjoyed their retirement together. Marion told me that in his later years he had a great love of doing jigsaw puzzles and when she visited him at Bedford she was never allowed to help him for as he told her "it's my puzzle and it would not be fair to let anyone help me". I dare say at the time Marion thought 'stubborn old so-and-so' but today she has fond memories of her parents and thanks them for teaching her that hard work will bring its rewards in the end. Her father died a short time before her mother and in Marion's words "he had a peaceful passing". Today Marion is still working hard and she told me it keeps her going, along with the love of her family.

All that remains for me to do is to thank Marion for sharing her story with us and to wish her many years of long life and happiness down at Great Lathe Farm. God bless and keep you safe Marion.

Footnote:
Marion has eight grandchildren and I could see the love she has for them as she spoke of them all so lovingly. They won't need me to tell them what a wonderful lady they have as their grandmother and I hope they will sit and talk to her about all the things she has seen and done, so that they can have an even better insight into her life.

"MY WAR EFFORT"
by Marion Andrews

In forty-one fate brought us here
To work and play and worry.
We left behind our families dear,
For England's name to carry.
We did not know what lay in store,
But knew we'd do our best,
With all our strength and evermore
For each there'd be no rest.
From early morn 'til late at night
In sun and rain, in wind and snow,
Our thresher worked with all its might
And us four girls just let it go.
Here comes Jerry! Let's dive for the ditch,
Low over the hedges he drops his load,
Narowly missing our threshing pitch,
Leaving its mark right up the road.
But five minutes later we're back with the seed,
There's work to be done, yes a War to be won.
An Army of men we need to feed,
A young child's father, or a mother's son
Have given their all for peace to be won.
Memories are precious, that no-one can steal,
As we sit and ponder and think of the past,
For now peace has come, we pray God it will last.

Joyce Todd's Story

The story you are about to read is the true story from another of our brave hard-working Land Army girls. I know how privileged I am that Joyce has allowed me to be the one to write her story for her. I shall never forget my first meeting with Joyce at her home in Cambridge. Although it was near to the end of June, it was a terrible day, with heavy rain all day long. As soon as I arrived Joyce put the coffee on and we settled back to chat about her wartime story over coffee and biscuits. As we looked over the photos and memorabilia that Joyce had from that time in her life, I knew I was in for a wonderful story. I was introduced to Joyce thanks to Mike Petty, a local historian who writes weekly articles for my local Cambridge Evening News. Mike was kind enough to cover an article for me, on the subject of Land Army girls from World War II. He also included my request for any of them who wanted their story included in my fourth book, to please get in touch. Mike called the article he did for me 'In Search of Hidden Warriors', a very apt title I think. Thankfully, Joyce read the article and offered any help she could on the subject, which all Land Army girls will know is so close to her heart. The following is Joyce's story.

Joyce was born and raised in Hucknal, Nottingham, and enjoyed life as children did in those days, by playing games like hopscotch, hide and seek, skipping etc, not like today with all the computer games and electronic gadgetry that we have in the nineties. Joyce was one of three children, having an older brother and a younger brother. Like us all, she still has fond memories of her childhood days, and she spoke proudly to me of her brothers and her parents. When war broke out Joyce was still at school, and was told not to worry as it would all soon be over. Little did she know then that it would be some six years later before peace would come to dear old England again. And, yes, at the cost of so many brave souls. Joyce's elder brother joined the army to do his bit for King and country and of course this was a constant worry for Joyce and her family but, as she said, they were not alone, for all around our great country, young men and women were leaving home to serve their country's need. There were not many familes that did not have a family member involved in the war effort. Before Joyce left school she had learnt that war had nothing nice to offer, except comradeship, for she had seen many families receive bad news from the War Department about a son or husband who was missing, believed killed in action. It was only thanks to friends and family and the support of the local community that people came through such nightmare times.

When Joyce became 18 years old, she was ready to do her bit for the war effort and so she and her friend joined the Women's Land Army – a day that was to change her life so much. Now it was goodbye to the city life and a big hello to rural England and all that went with it. Joyce and her friend were sent to the village of Impington to work on Chivers Farms, in Cambridgeshire (the village where I live today). After packing her kit bag and saying her goodbyes to her family, it was now her turn to face that big old world. She and her friend set off that day with great excitement in their hearts, as well as a feeling of sadness at leaving Hucknal, and all that had felt safe to them up until now. As their journey brought them nearer to Cambridge they sat and spoke to one another about their hidden fears of what life would be like for them. One thing they were both sure of is that it would be very hard work, for they knew enough to know that land work was far from easy. They arrived at the station in Histon, a village which shares its boundary with Impington, indeed many people think of the villages as one, with Histon on one side of the main road, and Impington on the other. They arrived on a very cold day in January 1944, and were met by one of Chivers Farms employees, and after collecting up their belongings they started their walk to what was now to be their new home.

Burgoynes House was a very large house which was owned by the Chivers family, and was now being used as a Land Army girls hostel. It was a good mile walk from the station and on such a cold winters day Joyce and her friend were glad that it was no further, as they felt dead on their feet from tiredness. Once the girls had been shown to their quarters they were told to leave their things and come and have a hot drink and something to eat. They were both pleased to hear this and gladly went off to be shown the forces canteen which was across the road from the hostel, in the new Impington College, which had been built on the site of the old Impington Hall, a very grand old building, as good as any grand stately home. For many of the older generation it was a sorry day when it was pulled down because of neglect. Its wonderful grand staircase was rotten with woodworm, as were the floorboards and joists etc. So many local people who grew up in the village after the First World War, and up until the 1930s, have happy memories of playing in the old house, even if their parents and the village bobby had told them "don't you dare go near that dangerous old building." My own mother has happy childhood memories of playing such games as Kings and Queens and Lord of the Manor etc. She recalls the very grand staircase as something like that used in the film "Gone with the Wind" in which Clark Gable and Vivien Leigh acted out that famous scene as Rhett Butler and Scarlett O'Hara. You may remember as he descended that grand staircase to leave he said, "Frankly, my dear, I don't give a damn". The Hall was the home of the Pepys family in the 16th century and Samuel Pepys was a regular visitor there when he visited his uncle Talbot Pepys and his cousin Roger Pepys, as Samuel states in his famous diaries. I feel that today's powers-that-be would never allow such a grand old building to be demolished. It has played its part in the history of the village of Impington and, as I say, to this day brings back happy memories to so many of the senior citizens who still live in the village.

Joyce and the other girls now with her were taken into the canteen, and were glad to receive a good hot meal and hot drink, and to be able to just sit and relax after their journey. As Joyce and the girls sat relaxing and enjoying their meal, a young airman introduced himself to them. He was Peter Todd, son of the Chivers Farms foreman from their farm at St. Ives, some eighteen miles away. Peter was a young pilot and Joyce just fell in love with him at first sight – he was so dashing and so good looking. Joyce couldn't remember much that was said to her for the rest of that day, as all she had on her mind now was her thoughts of Peter. As she said, she was on cloud nine and she knew at once that she had met the man she wanted to marry and spend the rest of her life with. The rest of the day soon passed and a very tired Joyce turned in for the night. Before she knew it, still deep in her dreams, she was quickly awoken by the sounds of the farm cockerels crowing for the start of a new day. Yes, it was 6.00am and time to start her working day. She quickly arose and went off for breakfast, then at 7.00am it was off to work. She and the other girls, who were mainly from the big cities of dear old England, were all wondering what to expect for they had only known city life up until now and most of them had only worked in shops etc. The morning was very cold with a very sharp frost to greet them, and as they stepped outside, their hot breath left a white vapour trail as they spoke to one another. The farm foreman soon got them warmed up with a brisk walk to the fruit orchards where they were put to work pruning the trees and clearing up all the dead and fallen branches. Winter work also meant clearing out the barns and the girls would load up large carts, drawn by horses of course. It was such hard work for the girls, but after a few weeks of backache and blistered hands, the girls found that they were developing muscles that they never even knew they had. They had all struck up a good working relationship by now and their comradeship was to make them become life long friends and although at the time they did not realize it, their friendships would go on to stand the test of time. Joyce and the girls looked forward to Saturday nights for there would be a dance to attend and the Army boys billeted at the college and the R.A.F. boys from the nearby airfields would all attend. Many of the girls were to meet their future husbands at these Saturday night dances, when a good time would be had by all. The only trouble is, they went far to quickly but they did generate enough gossip to last the girls all through the next week, talking to one another as they worked away side by side. Some of the girls were to fall in love with young airmen, but they knew they would have to live for the day, for they knew by now that the life of an airman could be a short one in times of war. Many of you will know that it was fraught with danger.

As the warmer weather came Joyce was kept busy planting out strawberry plants. To this day, Chivers Farms are known worldwide for their strawberries and, of course, their lovely strawberry jam, along with all their other mouth-watering delights. This was much lighter work, and after the hard winter days it was a happy time planting out, just to know that old Jack Frost would not be hurting your fingers. The warm weather was making everyone feel much better and although the girls didn't like their uniforms (they all say the uniform was a real passion-killer), now at last they could discard their winter coats and roll up their sleeves. When it came time to picking the strawberries, this was another job for the girls, and once again it was a back-aching job with very long days. Joyce recalls the 7.00am start and the 9.00pm finish, which were also the hours worked right through the harvest time. Once the strawberries were picked, the girls loaded them into wooden trays, then onto horse-drawn carts and on to the main Chivers factory, where they would also unload them ready for the jam making process. Harvest time was very hard work for the girls, and Joyce remembers having to work with German and Italian prisoners-of-war who were brought in from nearby prison camps to help with the work. Joyce recalls that the German prisoners were very helpful and would lift the heavy bales of straw for you, but the Italians would do all they could not to help you, and would be moaning all the time. On one occasion, after the fields had been ploughed up the Italian prisoners were asked to undertake muck-spreading of the fields, and asked to load up the horse-drawn carts with the muck from the pig farm, and cattle etc. This the Italians refused to do, and so this became another job for Joyce and the girls. As Joyce told me this story she laughed as she recalled the awful smell that the muck gave off, which seemed to eat into your clothes and hair and was not a very nice fragrance at all for ladies. As she said, those Italian prisoners were not daft in refusing to do it. I could not help but think of my own father and his comrades and wondered what their Japanese captors would have done to them if they had said "no, we won't build your bloody railway for you", or if my dad had said to that Jap executioner "no, I will not assist you in your work of death." Needless to say I would not have been here today, as my father's captors would not have been like the good old British were to the Italians.

On one of these summer evenings, Joyce was asked to go with the shepherd to Histon railway station, as a delivery of sheep was due in. Joyce went off with the shepherd to walk the mile to the station, where they helped unload the sheep from the cattle trucks.They then had the job of herding the sheep up and getting them to walk through the streets of the village back to the farm. Just across the road from the station there was a village shop and the sheep at the front of the flock walked up to the shop window and, on seeing their reflection in the window, caused quite a comotion as they didn't know whether they were coming or going, a feeling that Joyce now knew only to well. It brought back happy memories to Joyce, recalling her time spent helping the shepherd, and as she said, it was hard work getting the sheep back to the farm – so many of them had a mind of their own, and would drift off into peoples' gardens to munch away at what ever they could find to eat. The locals would call out "you get them bloody sheep out of my garden" to which Joyce would shout back "I'm doing my best to do just that, sir". Needless to say, the sheep did eventually get to the farm, much to Joyce's delight.

Joyce had now started working with the animals and most of the girls had only heard of cows until now, but now they were being asked to milk them! Some thought they only had to pump the cows tail up and down to do this, but they were soon to learn it was not that easy, although once they were shown, they soon got the hang of it. Of course, many of the girls got the pail of milk kicked over them by the cow just as they had got it full. The girls soon learnt which cows to watch out for, and many of them would sing to the cows to calm them, although if the other girls didn't like your singing you can imagine the remarks that were made. But it was all in good fun, and if nothing else, war does bring good comradeship, and Joyce and the girls were finding this to be so true. One job Joyce was given to do made a nice change from the work on the land. She had to ride an old type of bike, like the ones ice cream sellers had at that time – the ones with the big delivery baskets on the front, from which they would shout out 'stop me and buy one'. Joyce would have to load up the front of the bike with home made meat pies, then bike to the main Chivers factory and around the farms and sell the pies to those who wanted them for lunch etc. As all Land Army girls will know, they really did have to be jacks-of-all-trades, and Joyce recalled what a great learning time it was for her, for she was now doing things she would never forget and things that would stand her in good stead in the years to come.

When VE Day came, Joyce was given leave and travelled home on the night train to Nottingham. There were no seats available so Joyce and the girls had to sit on the soldiers' laps, but they told her they didn't mind at all, and as Joyce said "being honest, we girls also thought it was good fun". There was plenty of singing and merryment had by all, the night soon passed, and Joyce found herself back in Nottingham ready to join in the activities surrounding the VE celebrations. It was a time so many had dreamed of for so very long and they all now hoped that the war in the Far East would also soon be over. Joyce remembered back to her school days, some six years before, when she had been told "don't worry dear, it will soon all be over". Six years later, here she was, celebrating at last. She met many of her old friends and neighbours, and soon found that so many of them had lost a dear loved one while they had been doing their bit for King and country. Although it was a time they all had prayed for, so many still had a loved one away overseas, and they knew they couldn't really celebrate until they were home and all together once again, alas a thing that was not to be for so many families. Joyce heard people say on numerous occasions throughout the celebrations, "now we've got those Nazis sorted out, we can show those Japs what for", but, as we know, it took two 'A' bombs to do that. So many brave Nottingham men were saved from death as prisoners of the Japanese owing to these two bombs, as were so many from around our homeland. Tragic as it was, it did give us younger ones our lives today.

Joyce attended lots of dances and parties while at home on leave – it was such a happy time. It also gave her time to charge her batteries, so to speak, and prepare herself for her return to the hard work that was still waiting for her, back on the farms. Britain now had to rebuild, and to do this the farms would have a very important role to play in providing good food to feed our brave war heroes who were now to face the task of making our country great again. Joyce soon found her leave coming to an end and said her goodbyes once again to her mother and father and her immediate family, and set off back to Impington to restart her work. One day in July, Joyce went into the forces canteen and once again saw Peter, and as their eyes met it really was love at first sight for both of them, and, as they say, the rest is history, for as you already know, Joyce's surname is Todd, but it would not be fair of me if I did not share the rest of this wonderful story with you, even if many of you have read of wartime romance before. Joyce and Peter chatted away as if they had known one another for years. They found that they were at ease with one another right from the start, and when the other girls called out "come on Joyce, we must get back to work", it was all dear Joyce could do to pull herself away, for all she now wanted was to be with Peter. The other girls were now asking all about him, and Joyce told them how Peter was taking her to the dance on Saturday and that they would all be able to chat to him then. She also told them how pleased she was that Peter would be able to see her in a proper dress at last and not in her Land Army passion-killers, to which some of the girls said "it's probably the uniform that has drawn him to you", at which they all had a good laugh. The Saturday dance was never to be forgotten, for their love for one another just grew and grew, and just 9 weeks after they met they became engaged. They met on the 9th of September, on the 9th November they were engaged, and 9 months later on 9th June they were married. Joyce told me how Peter's plane was even known as number 9 and looking back she realized how important the number 9 had been to them in their lives. Peter had now received orders that he would soon be going out to the war in the Far East and, as we have said before, one had to live for the day, and I am sure this played a big part in their decision to get married. They were so much in love and wanted to just be together as man and wife like so many other couples had done before them, but as so many ladies know to their cost, so many of those who became wartime brides were to become war widows.

Joyce told me how when she told her mother she was getting married, she said "Joyce, I won't be able to get everything sorted out in time. With this war on and what with the rations it's going to be hard". Joyce smiled at her mother and said "you don't have to worry about a thing, mother. Peter and I will sort everything out. All we want you and dad to do is just to be there for us with our friends and family and enjoy yourselves". Her mother replied "oh, I think we can manage that love". When the wedding day arrived it was a wonderful day and, needless to say, there were none prouder than Joyce's parents, as Joyce and Peter were married in Mary Magdalene Church, Hucknall, the same church that holds the remains of Lord Byron in his family vault. Not long after the wedding, Peter was moved up north for more training, for he had been told he would now be going to fight the Japanese. This was not a happy time for Joyce as you can imagine – she knew that pilots flying against the Japanese at this time had a very short life expectancy. They were given about 14 days at most, for as many of you will know, the Japanese fighter pilots didn't mind if they lived or died, as long as they served their Emperor, hence the phrase "Kamikaze Pilots" – those who just set their planes on a collision course with their target, which many of our sailors, as well as our airmen, still have nightmares about to this day. It was also, of course, a very worrying time for Peter, for here he was, a newly married man knowing only too well how Joyce would be worring about him, but he also knew he had to do his best for King and country and so he put his heart and soul into his training and hoped and prayed that he would be one of the lucky ones and survive it all. At this time Peter often got sent to an aerodrome near to Hucknall which was mainly manned by Polish airmen. When Joyce heard this, she put in for a transfer to Nottingham and was soon given a position working for the Sheriff of Nottingham's estate, which was so very large. Joyce thought she had learnt all about hard work while on the Chivers farms back in Impington, but here she was given so much to do that she really did find that there were not enough hours in the day for her. She was able to live at home with her mum and dad now, but this meant a five mile bike ride to work and back each day. She recalled that one of the worst jobs that she had to do was after the Sherriff and his guests had undertaken a shoot on the estate, and all the pheasants had to be hung for about three to four weeks, until they were really ripe, after which she would have to pluck and draw them, ready for cooking. She said you needed a clothes peg on your nose while you undertook this task, to prevent you passing out from the awful smell. She also had four nice jersey milking cows to look after, and with their milk she made butter etc. If she was lucky, now and again she would get a Saturday afternoon off which, if possible, she would spend with her darling Peter. Peter played a lot of sport for the R.A.F., and Joyce often found herself being the scorer at a cricket match on her valuable afternoons off, or if not, watching Peter play hockey. She told me how she didn't mind though, for at least she was near to him.

When August arrived Peter was at last ready for the off, and was on stand by to go to the Far East. As the day of his departure approached, news came through that the Americans had dropped atom bombs on Japan so Peter and his chums could stand down, and would now not have to go. You can imagine what a great relief this must have been for both of them, it really was a dream come true for Joyce to know that her Peter would not have to go, and as we know, not too long after the atom bombs falling, Japan at last surrendered. At last the victory was won. VJ Day came with partying and dancing for all. After six years of heartache, and much hardship, life hopefully could now get back to normal. Alas, though, for so many, their lives would never be the same again.

Even though Joyce was allowed time away from the estate on a Saturday afternoon she still had to turn up each day to milk the cows, and make sure the other animals were fed. She even had to do this when Peter was home on leave, which she hated when she was having so much fun with Peter, but, as she said, animals can't be left – they really need to be fed and cared for around the clock. You can't say to them "milk yourselves today please." So as you can see, it really was seven days a week for our Land Army girls, a thing I am sure that many of our farmers will know only to well today. Joyce carried on working at the Sherriffs estate, but after a few months the strain of everything was really beginning to affect her health. The work was still so very hard and the hours long, and she had started to lose so much weight that everyone was worried about what was wrong with her and so her days as a Land Army girl were brought to an end.

Once Peter had left the R.A.F., he wanted to return to be near his parents and friends back in Impington, so he and Joyce returned to Cambridgeshire and set up home together. Peter found himself a job as a designer draughtsman at Unicam, in Cambridge, which in later years was taken over by Pye, where Peter was to spend his working life. Joyce and Peter's happiness was made complete with the birth of their daughter Helen, and once again Joyce recalled that she had been told she would be born on the 9th and Joyce feels sure this would have been the case if they had not started her labour the day before, so needless to say Helen was born on the 8th. Yes, it took the British medical midwives to stop Joyce and Peter's run of nines, but Joyce said it will always be a special number for her. As the years passed and Helen grew she inherited her parents' love for dancing and of course was the apple of her father's eye. Joyce told me of how as a baby, Helen would be in her carrycot under the the table while Joyce scored the cricket match for Peter and his team. Peter loved his cricket and played for the village of Stapleford in Cambridgeshire, and also for his works team at Pye.

In 1995, Joyce and Peter celebrated their 50th wedding anniversary – a wonderful day when all Peter's old R.A.F. chums, and Joyce's Land Army girls all came and shared their special day with them. It was also a special year for our great country. Yes, 1995 – fifty years since the war ended. As Peter and Joyce danced together that evening they smiled at one another as they gave thanks to God for the wonderful life they had shared together. All those years ago, with all the upset of war going on around them, never could they have imagined that they would be just as happy and still so much in love some fifty years on. Sadly, soon after this wonderful day, Peter was taken from us to make his last trip or flight to that far better place that awaits such brave souls in paradise. Joyce is left with fifty years of wonderful happy memories but it is those war time memories, and the memory of the very first time she set eyes on her darling Peter that are still as strong in her mind today as they were all those years ago. Every time she spoke to me of Peter, I could see that her love for him was as strong now as it was on the very first day that they had met.

Today Joyce is kept busy helping her daughter Helen, who is a professional dancer, and dance teacher. Joyce has two grandaughters Amanda and Sarah, who are also both very good dancers and have many shields and cups and badges to prove it (I think it must be in the blood you know). I could see how proud Joyce was of her girls, as she showed me how busy they kept her, making their lovely costumes and hats etc, for the dance productions that they take part in. I dont think Helen and the girls will need me to tell them how proud they can be of Joyce, and I am sure that like me they know how important a part she played in giving us younger ones our today, for like all Land Army girls, Joyce played her part in keeping the home fires burning while our men were away fighting for our tomorrow.

Joyce has now had to adapt to life alone but has the love of her daughter and grandaughters to help her through life's journey. She told me how there are not many days that she does not get to see them. She also plays an active part in her village and also stays in touch with the pensioners from Pye, where her Peter worked for so long and she says she never has time to get bored. Life is for living, and I say "long may she be able to do just that."

All that remains for me to say is a big thankyou to Joyce for sharing her story with us and an even bigger thank you for what she gave for our today.

Footnote:
As I was about to say goodbye to Joyce and leave her to carry on making her girls' costumes, I asked her what memory stuck in her mind most about the end of the war. She told me that it would be while working on Chivers farm at St. Ives in Cambridgeshire (which in those days would have been part of Huntingdonshire). It was near to VE Day or very soon after, when Joyce had returned from Nottingham. Mr. Thomson, the farm manager at St. Ives, asked everyone to gather round the farm

flag pole. This included the German prisoners-of-war. He asked for two minutes silence to remember those who had given the ultimate sacrifice. He then asked the German prisoners-of-war to raise the Union Jack and all sing 'God save the King'. This the German prisoners gladly did, and after this small private ceremony, the German prisoners told Joyce and the other girls just how pleased they were that peace had come at last. They spoke of how they longed to see their loved ones again and to stand once again in their homeland, for which they were not afraid to shed a tear. They then told Joyce a thing that I say many times when doing my talks and wartime programmes – yes, they told her that war is no good, for it is the innocent, hard-working, ordinary people who really suffer and they knew now that war was not the answer. I myself have said before in my books "WILL MANKIND EVER LEARN"? I just hope and pray that they can for we must make sure that such things are never allowed to happen again. We must all work hard for worldwide peace, and offer the hand of friendship to all nationalities, and make our planet earth a real great place to live.

In pride of place in Joyce's home today, hangs a wonderful painting depicting the scene of an English field at harvest time. It has Peter's aeroplane flying over the field and in the foreground are Peter and Joyce, both in their wartime uniforms. It is truly a wonderful painting that truly holds the key to a wonderful love story.

Marion Andrews on the farm

Marion, Ruby, Betty and Joan with their new Land Army bikes

Marion (middle) in Land Army uniform

Marion and John on their Wedding day

Joyce Todd (back row third on right) at Chivers Farm, Impington, Cambridge

Joyce and Peter Todd

*Joyce and Peter Todd on their
Wedding day*

*Topsy Price in a photo used for a
recruiting poster*

Minty Upsall (front row right), Chester

Minty Upsall (back row right) at Abbey Raod Hostel at Rhuddlan, which is now a caravan site Club House

Minty Upsall (left) Porthcawl, Autumn 1949 trainees from Ross on Wye

Topsy Price working at Croes Bleddyn Farm, Chepstow.(1940)

Topsy Price in a photograph from the Daily Express, August 1943 after returning from Buckingham Palace to meet the Royal Family

Joan Wallis working on the farm

The following true story comes from Mrs. Dorothy G. Pitfield from Nottingham, who wrote to me in June 1997 with her wartime story after hearing a programme that I did on BBC Radio Nottingham, on the subject of War Time Women. She told me how, after the war, she wrote down a rather unusual story that she herself had taken part in. She explained to me that reading through it some 52 years since the end of World War II, it struck her as a very light-hearted account, but, as she says, it needed a very concentrated, intensive effort from so many dedicated people, to bring success. The following is her story.

The Tyburn Operation

"In January 1945, I was serving as a member of the Womens' Auxillary Territorial Service, and I was stationed with a heavy Ack-Ack battery on the east coast. The battery was charged with shooting down the V1s, commonly called buzz bombs, which the Germans were at that time launching from Holland across the North Sea. Our guns were attempting to destroy them over the sea before they could wreak their devastation on this island. It was a bitterly cold winter with several inches of snow on the ground, and I must admit, with some feelings of relief, I learned from the A.T.S. Officer in charge that I was to be posted the next day. However, this posting was apparently a mystery to everyone. "Have you applied for remustering" queried the officer. "No" I replied. "Well," said she, "your posting has come by telegram from the War Office, and tomorrow you are to report to The Golf House, The Golf Links, Tadworth, Surrey. Here are your posting instructions, and railway warrant. Make sure you catch the train as stated".

"Consequently, with those brief instructions, I packed my kit bag, and turned in for an early night, ready for the journey next day. On arriving at London Bridge station on the last stage of my journey to Tadworth, my attention was drawn to another A.T.S. girl apparently waiting for the same train. In the usual spirit of camaraderie which seems to exist only in times of stress or war, we approached each other, and on exchanging notes we were both apparently bound for the same destination, which helped dispel a feeling of loneliness. There were other coincidences, for we were both medical orderlies and had been summoned in a similar manner – by War Office telegram. Her officer was seemingly better informed than mine, for she told my companion we were bound for some highly secret occupation. This information had the effect of stimulating our imaginations to the limit. By the time we reached Tadworth, the exciting and varied prospects discussed were numerous. On our arrival at the Golf House, I, plus approximately thirty other travel-stained, bewildered girls who had arrived from units in various parts of the country, were conveyed by lorry to a large Victorian mansion, which was to be our living quarters for the next few days. My chief memory of this ancient lodging was the bathroom and constant hot water, a very rare luxury in those days. On entering the bathroom to indulge in this heaven-found luxury, I was dazzled and astounded by the decor – evidently the Victorians who could afford it really bathed in style. The bath was like a miniature marble swimming pool, with elegant steps leading down into the water, and a carved water nymph at either side, with which to steady oneself. It took some time to discover which ornaments were taps, and how to turn them on, and that the swan's head was the top of the plug, which dropped into place when the beak was turned in a certain direction. I then searched for that other piece of necessary bathroom equipment, and was just deciding that the people of that day and age must delight in extremes, and after bathing in luxury, must then have resorted to a garden privy, when my attention was drawn to a scarlet plush padded armchair, indeed, almost a throne. Ah, yes, discreetly, cunningly hidden in the centre of the plush, a trapdoor. Oh, what heaven."

"The next morning and for the following few days my companions and I presented ourselves at the Golf House, where we carried out a series of tests, which were evidently for the purpose of discovering our IQs. The following day was taken up by a thorough medical examination, but still no hint of what was in store for us. We left the golf links at Tadworth, and arrived this time at Lingfield holding unit. I knew from past experience how boring, and pointless, these holding units seemed to be. One could stay for weeks, doing nothing but a few fatigues (chores). However, this time we were fortunate – we were informed that an interview had been arranged for us at the War Office, on the following day."

"We duly arrived at Hobart House, Victoria. The security paraphernalia we passed through before being admitted was an experience in itself. Nevertheless, we were finally allowed through those well guarded porticos, and followed our escort down innumerable passages, until at last we arrived outside a room with our code number on the door. After waiting an interminable time, the door opened and one of our number was requested to enter. Eventually came my turn.... was I now to hear details of my own future occupation at last? I found myself in a large room, with a long table running down the centre of it, and turned towards me what seemed like a sea of faces. The army officer seated at the head of the table was evidently the spokesman. He proceeded to ask me my life history right from my childhood to the present day. I answered as clearly as possible, after which I was dismissed, and returned to my compatriots, none the wiser for my interview. At long last the individual interviews came to an end. We were once again invited into the room, this time all together. The officer at the head of the table rose to his feet, and as far as my memory serves this is what he said. "The operation in which you have been selected to take part will be explained to you shortly, but first of all I must tell you there is a certain element of risk attached, and when everything has been explained, you will then be asked to volunteer, but if any of you have no wish to take part, you may stand down. You must all, in the best interests of your country, swear to secrecy, and discuss this with no one, not even your own families. We all know with gratitude, the war in Europe is progressing favourably, but that is not your war from now on. Yours is in the Far East, fighting the Japanese in the jungles of Burma. Unbeknown to most people, our greatest enemy, yes our greatest common enemy, because it also affects the Japanese, is a tiny mite which stalks the jungles – almost microscopic, yet its bite brings death to many in the form of scrub typhus. This disease is causing more deaths on both sides than the enemy action at this time. A team of our scientists have perfected a vaccine to protect our men against this scourge. You understand the reason for utmost secrecy, for no word of this must reach the Japanese, as this vaccine is equivalent to a new weapon in our hands. You, together with a team of doctors and scientists, will manufacture this vaccine. The name of this operation will be 'Tyburn' ". After swearing to secrecy we filed silently from the room. My feelings were mixed. This certainly wasn't the type of work I'd envisaged, but if it meant helping to save these valiant mens' lives, what could I do but volunteer? We returned to the holding unit to await our instructions. There was not long to wait. Soon four other girls and myself were sent to the National Institute of Medical Research at Hampstead, to begin our training."

"It was a very impressive building, many stories high. On our first morning we were shown around, and very interesting it all was. I was busy speculating as to which of these wonderfully-equipped laboratories I would be working, when we emerged from the lift on the top floor. A peculiar odour met our nostrils – one that would become very familiar to us in the future, had we but known. This floor was different from the others; here was bare concrete, obviously recently swilled down, and very damp, with doors on either side. The sight of a pile of cages gave me a clue – yes, animals were involved. An amiable looking man met us in the passageway, and our escort said, 'meet our chief animal technician. I will leave you now in his capable hands'. 'Why leave us with the animals?' we thought. Surely our work was to be in the laboratories, a far more glamourous prospect than this odorous atmosphere."

"We were shown some white mice, then rabbits, docile guinea pigs, and even monkeys. Then the animal technician opened a door and stood aside for us to enter, but the heat and stench which met us was just overwhelming. Not liking to show the reluctance we felt, we held our breath, and entered. I gazed around. It was quite a small room, lined with cages which appeared empty, apart from sawdust on the floors, and also a piece of drainpipe in each of them. At the end of the room stood an ordinary dustbin. Where was the dreadful smell emanating from? The stifling heat seemed to rise in waves, as indeed it did, as we discovered later at the cost of our feet, for the heating came from the floor."

"Now these animals," said our instructor with great pride, indicating the apparently empty cages, "are cotton rats, from the cotton fields in South America. They are very delicate, and temperamental, and, I might add, quite viscious creatures. They take a violent dislike to being handled, and if not handled correctly will give you a very nasty bite. They hide in the drain pipes which you can see in the cages, the nearest thing we can provide to their natural habitat. It is my duty to instruct you in the care of handling, and general husbandry of these animals, also to initiate you into the mysteries of sex determination of them, which can only be carried out with accuracy shortly after birth."

"Was this then to be our great war effort? By then I was feeling quite sick and faint. How on earth could I face working in such an atmosphere, apart from having to deal with these loathsome creatures? Magically we were soon completely at home, with what were by now our rats. They had aroused in us a healthy respect for their craft, and swift action, as our bitten fingers proclaimed, if not our affection. Within a very few weeks we were very efficient cotton rat nurses, having learnt their likes and dislikes, their culinary and otherwise amusing quirks of behaviour. For example, if one escaped from a cage or bin, we at first, in our ignorance, would attemp to grasp it by the tail, which would promptly come off in your hand, while the rat continued on it's way."

"I also now understand the part we were playing in the Tyburn operation. It appears the only animal in which the rickettsia, (that is the organism which causes the disease) will grow successfully is in the lungs of a cotton rat. Therefore hundreds of these creatures were required before the actual production could begin. We five were to be the pioneers. Along with a few male and female rats, which were to be flown to us from South America, we were to start a breeding unit to supply the laboratories with the rats necessary for the quantities of vaccine needed."

"One foggy day we left London without regret, for the V2s had started their bombardment of the city, and life there was not a bed of roses. We arrived at our final destination, a lovely house set in beautiful grounds in Sussex – a peaceful haven after life in London. By the morning the fog had lifted, and we could really appreciate the pleasant scenery surrounding us. To say I was surprised is an understatement when, on exploring the working site, I discovered hundreds of engineers busily digging the foundations of the laboratories. I wondered 'were we now to kick our heels and wait for the buildings to be completed?' Fortunately not. On the far side of the site was a long building, a disused piggery so we were informed. This then was to be our breeding house, once all the necessary alterations hade been made, and heating had been installed. Soon it was finished, and our first consignment of cotton rats arrived at London airport in specially heated planes. They were collected and rapidly conveyed to Sussex before they could come to any harm. We then started work in earnest."

"Each week the laboratories grew like magic, the engineers worked all the hours possible. The number of rats increased, and the number of staff increased, until finally in the spring, with the laboratories completed we were at full production. When the big event of VE Day came in May, we were once again reminded that this was not our victory, ours had still to come. We drank to the peace in Europe with orange juice and salt tablets, all that was available to us, and then continued on with our work. We had by now all been vaccinated with the vaccine which we were helping to produce. We wore rope soled sandals, and tropical kit, whilst at work, for the temperature in the rattery was often over 100° F. The entomologist checked up each day on our charges, on the number of births etc. We were warned to take our salt tablets daily, because of the heat, and the loss of perspiration that we were suffering. Efficiency rose, and I found that being so much in contact with the cotton rats had made us as swift in action as they were. If one escaped, no longer was a pipe laid as a trap, for as soon as a rat leapt from a cage or bin, the hand would unerringly land on the back of the neck of the rat and gripping the fur so that the head and legs were rigid, no longer were our fingers chewed to bits. Three of our number became infected with scrub typhus, but the vaccine proved itself and they recovered completely after a short spell in the hospital. Rumours in the village ran riot among the local inhabitants; the tales were many and varied, but the truth of what we were doing never leaked out. Eventually VJ Day came, and we celebrated fully this time, making up for not being involved in the VE Day celebrations, but it was also with a sense of anticlimax, for production ceased, everything was disbanded, and once more we were redundant and awaiting new postings."

"I left Sussex for a new unit in Devon with a sharp pang of regret at leaving the many friends I had made. It had been a united, harmonious community, as indeed was necessary for such an intensive, concerted effort as TYBURN."

"Now all these years on I look back with such pride, at the way I helped my fellow man, and my King and country, when I played my part as a " War Time Woman".

Author's reply:
Dear Dorothy, Thank you so very much for sharing your wonderful story with us and for allowing me to tell it here in my book, 'War Time Women'. Like the other ladies' stories in this book, we the readers can

see the debt of gratitude that we owe to you all for the part you have all played in giving us our today. I would also like to thank you on behalf of my dear late father and his comrades, and also for the men of the 14th Army who fought and suffered in the jungles of Burma, and the rest of the Far East. The vaccine that you helped to bring about would have gone to ensure that these very brave men lived to fight another day, and I am sure for many it meant the difference between life and death. The conditions that you worked in and the great humid heat, as you will know, was to match the conditions that these men found themselves in, so you will know better then most, just what it was really like for them.

Yours thankfully,
Michael Bentinck.

FOR HOME AND COUNTRY

Arise, oh women of England,
Now that the war is won,
You carried on for the men while they had gone,
But your work is just begun.
Nobly you did your duty,
In hospital, factory and field,
And you showed your grit, and did your bit,
To make the enemy yield.
But it rests with the women of England now,
As they think of the sons they have lost,
To see that their homes and their country
Are worthy of the price they have cost.

Mary Chambers' Story

Our next story comes from Miss Mary Chambers of Lincolnshire. Mary is another lady who was proud to play her part for King and country, by serving in the Women's Land Army. She told me how much she enjoyed hearing my wartime memories programme on BBC Radio Lincolnshire with my presenter friend, Melvyn Prior. Sadly, before I could bring this book out, Mary has gone to take her place in that big harvest in heaven, but before she died she asked me to please include her story. The following is Mary's story.

"I was a Land Army girl and was proud to play my part in the war effort. I worked on many farms across our great country, and met all types of people from all walks of life. The story I want to share with you is what happened while I was working on a farm in Wales, near to Hereford, along with four other girls, plus a mixture of farm labourers and pensioners and, towards the end of the war, even some prisoners-of-war. It was so very hot at the height of summer, we were all getting the harvest in and we made a pretty sight with our trouser bottoms tied up with string, such was our fear of the mice and rats running up our legs, which was quite a common thing when cutting the corn down. It was such hard work and very long hours, with an 8.00am start, and it was nothing to work until 10.00pm in the evening. It was a very dusty job, as it is to this day, when the weather is hot and dry, and it is still not a very lady-like job, although I believe many ladies still enjoy farming work today. On one particular day, during lunch break, which was around midday, one of the girls said 'I know where there are two old tin baths hanging up in the old cow shed, back at the farm yard.' She suggested that we put them at the rear of the main barn, where there was an old water pump over a well that had been on the farm for centuries, and fill them up with clear cold water, strip off, and have a nice refreshing soak. This sounded like heaven to me, for I was so hot and sweaty and of course was covered in dust from head to foot. We knew the men always sat and had their lunch together, just sitting on the straw near to where we were working. So we knew that they would not be about the farm yard. As soon as our boss blew his whistle to sound lunch break my friend Ivy and I set off for the farm yard, we got the two old tin baths from the cow shed and placed them behind the barn, and quickly pumped that fresh cool water into them. We then built up a shield around us by using some straw bales that lay at the rear of the barn, so that no one would see us. We then stripped off naked and I can still remember how good that cool water felt. We were both only 19 years old and had never had to work so hard in our lives. As we lay back relaxing in the cool water, we heard a tractor come into the yard, the engine stopped, and we could hear voices. Ivy looked towards me and said 'keep still and don't make a sound and they will go away'. Oh, how I prayed they would. I then heard a voice right near to us on the other side of the straw bales call out 'there's more bales of straw here gov'nor. The reply came back to him, 'well don't just look at them, load them onto the trailer then'. Imagine my thoughts as the bales of straw that we had placed around us suddenly started disappearing. We lay there not daring to say a word, or even to move. Then as this farm labourer lifted one of the bales he spotted us. His face lit up for he sure had a birds eye view. We screamed and put our hands across our breasts, and with that the farmer came running over to look as well. We had nothing to dry ourselves with, only our dusty old clothes, for if we had not been disturbed we planned to just lay in the sun and dry off. The two men just stood staring for what seemed like ages to us, so in the end we just jumped up, grabbed our clothes and ran into the old cow shed, quickly put our clothes back on and ran back to the fields as quickly as we could. Days later the farmer told us we could take a bath at the rear of the barn any time we liked, as he did not mind at all. We had learnt our lesson though, and told him firmly 'thank you, but no thank you'. We were never allowed to forget this incident, and were to blush at it many times when we went into the village, to the pub, or to the local dance. I remember not long afterwards we were at the local hop, when a couple of soldiers were trying to chat up Ivy and me, and kept wanting to buy us drinks. We didn't take to them at all – we had already said to one another 'they certainly think that they are God's gift to women don't they?' Well they kept trying to split us up when we were on the dance floor, and when one tried the wandering hands, I quickly hit out at him. Jack, the farm labourer who had seen us in the tin baths not long before, was there and came over to help us. He shouted at the young soldiers to behave themselves, and not to be so rude. He got punched in the face for his trouble, and the thing I heard the young soldier shout at him then upset me so much, as it does when I think of what he said to this day. He shouted at the top of his voice to Jack, 'we know all about these Land Army girls mate, what do you think W.L.A. stands for?' Before Jack could answer him, he shouted out 'yes, it stands for We Lay Anywhere!' Well, that was it. Ivy and I weighed into these two squaddies with our fists blazing out. I would like to think that they knew they had met their match in us girls for they just ran out, and we never saw them again. Later Jack said to us 'my God, I'm glad I never got any ideas that day I found you in the tin baths. I think you would have hit me a sight harder than that soldier did'. Ivy and I thanked him though, for stepping in to help us, and from that day on he became a real friend to us both, and saw to it that we kept out of trouble, so much so that in time Ivy fell madly in love with him, and in 1947 they were married. And I bet you can guess who was the chief bridesmaid! It was a wonderful day and I was proud to be there for Ivy and Jack and to share in their special day. As for me, I now to had to plan my future, for the war had brought its share of heartache to me – my home in London had been flattened in the blitz, sadly while my dear mum and dad were in the house. I was told they had been in bed together at the time, so at least they were together until the end. I was an only child and will never forget how loving they were to me. When I was given compassionate leave to go home to London to sort things out, I must admit that when I arrived at the end of our street and saw what was our row of houses just laying in a pile of brick rubble, I thought to myself 'what a joke, to tell me I was going home', for my childhood home now consisted of a pile of rubble".

"Once I had sorted things out I stayed one night in a London hotel as a treat to myself, and that night when I went down for dinner, I saw this dashing young airman also on his own. He asked me if I was dining alone and when I told him that I was, he asked me if I would do him the honour of joining him. I remember I put my best voice on, for I was already wearing my one and only dress, and replied that the honour would be all mine. I remember it was a wonderful evening and we felt so at ease with one another. As we chatted, he told me how he had been shot down over the channel, and was on leave at the moment to sort out his father's funeral. I told him the story of my dear mum and dad, and he was so kind and understanding, for of course I broke down in tears as I told him all about it. He held me in his arms and I felt safe for the first time in a very long while. He explained that at least his father had died of old age, and had been over 80. After dinner we sat in the lounge and had coffee and I remember he had this small silver hip flask containing brandy, which we shared by mixing it in with our coffee, (to this day I still enjoy brandy in my coffee). He was such a kind young man, David was his name, and I think it fair to say that I had fallen for him already, so after our coffee and drinks when he asked to escort me to my room, I allowed him to do so. Once at the door of my room he took me in his arms again and kissed me with such passion that I think I melted in his arms. He then just picked me up and took me into my room; it was something like a scene from a film, and I wondered if I was dreaming, but if it was a dream I must say that it was one of the best dreams that I have ever had, for all that night we made love, and when I awoke in the morning I found I was still lying in David's arms. We went down to breakfast, and of course the other guests looked at us as if we had guilt written all over our faces. But later, over breakfast, when I mentioned what must they all be thinking, David said to me 'Mary, they will be thinking 'what a lovely young wife that airman has'.' I think that made me blush even more, but what happened next caused me to go scarlet.... for David said, 'Mary will you marry me?' I was stunned and blurted out 'but David, I know nothing about you, and you know nothing of me'. He smiled back at me and said 'I don't need to, my love. All I know is that I love you and want to be with you for the rest of my life'. Well, that one night turned into three nights that we spent together, and when we left one another to return to play our parts in the great war effort, it was a very sad morning indeed – we were both in tears. We had exchanged addresses and promised to keep in touch by writing to one another until we could be together again."

"Once I arrived back in Wales, I told Ivy, who said 'good for you, Mary'. I must have driven her mad with my days of talking about nothing other than David. She was now courting with Jack, and when I look back I don't think I ever gave her a chance to tell me of what she and Jack were doing when not working with me on the farm. I met David whenever I could after this, and would save all my money for train fares, or even hitch a lift with a man from the village who took produce up to London. I was so in love with David and wanted to be with him all the time really, but the ruddy war was really getting in the way of that, but so many of my friends told me 'just live for today, Mary, and enjoy the time you can be together.' One day back on the farm, I was called over by our boss while working in the fields and asked to come with him back to the farm house. I asked what for, and was informed that someone wanted to see me. It was now the summer of 1944, and once again so very hot. I asked the boss 'who would come all this way to see me', for I had no family left except for an old aunt living in Spalding in Lincolnshire. The boss replied 'it's a young airman and he's driving a smashing open-top sports car'. I at once thought 'oh, it's David'. My heart was in my mouth, for all I could think of was what he would think of me dressed in my dungarees – he had only ever seen me in my best dress up to now. As we approached the farmhouse I saw the car, and the boss said to me 'if this here car belongs to your young airman, Mary me girl, then you really have done well for yourself'. I remember I said to my boss, 'whats a chap's car got to do with it?', but I have of course learnt as my life has gone on, that some men think more of their cars than they do their women. As soon as I stepped into the kitchen, this young airman jumped up. It was not David. He introduced himself as Clive, and said 'I am a good friend of David's. We are in the same squadron'. I replied 'oh, is David not with you?' to which he said 'Mary, please come and sit down'. Well as soon as he said that, I knew it was bad news, and I could detect it in his tone of voice. He said 'Mary, I have some very bad news for you, and there is no way that I can soften the blow for you. Yes, David is dead'. I of course was now crying uncontrollably, but he went on to say that David had spoken of nothing else but me since he first met me in London. He told me how David had been shot down in a raid over Germany. I said 'well perhaps he is a prisoner-of-war then'. I knew what Clive was going to say by the look on his face, even before his reply came back to me. He said 'Mary, I saw his plane get hit. He had no chance. The plane just burst into flames. He never had time to bale out, and to be honest, Mary, I think it was very quick for him'. I was in such a state of shock, but Clive told me to try to think of the good times we had shared together. He told me how David had told them all how he planned to marry me. He gave me a locket that I knew David sometimes wore, that contained a photo of his mum and dad, but when I opened it, there inside was a photo of me – one that I remembered David taking on one of our weekend meets together. Clive told me that he had an aunt in Worcester, not far from where we were, and he took me to stay with her for a few days. It really did help as she had met and known David a lot longer than I had, and we spoke of him together, which I know helped me so much at this very sad time in my life."

"Now back to 1947.... Ivy and Jack were married, and I had to move on with my life. As I had no home or parents to go home to, I decided that I would go and live with my aunt in Spalding. She had been made a young widow in the First World War, so I felt sure she would know how I was feeling at my loss of David. This is what I did and so came to live in Lincolnshire, but I never forgot my friends, especially Ivy and Jack, with whom I have spent many happy holidays. I also kept in touch with Clive's aunt in Worcester, until she died in the seventies. As for me, I never married, as I could never replace my love for David, and I know one day we will meet again in paradise, where such things as war and hatred will all be left behind in the world of the living. I myself am not afraid of death for I know it will take me to my true love once more."

"If nothing else, I hope that my story will show that in times of war there are such things as love, and amusing times like my tin bath incident, as well as the horrific things that war can bring.

Author's comments:

Dear Reader, As you will have read, dear Mary has departed our planet earth, and like her I hope and pray that she is with her dear hero David in paradise, where they can be happy together. I know how lucky I am to have spoken with Mary during her life. It would have made her so happy to know that her story has been told here, for she thought I wouldn't use it as it contained the tin bath incident. I hope, like me, you feel it has been our privilege to be able to read Mary's story, and it has been a great honour for me to write it. My God she knew the heartache that war brings, along with the lighter side of it. But to lose your parents and your sweetheart, as so many did of course, has really touched me. To Mary, and people like her who suffered so much in those dark days, I say thank you so much for what you all went through for us younger ones to have a life today.

"Rest in peace Mary"

Dora Ellis' Story

Our next story comes from Dora Ellis of Birmingham. Thankfully, Dora heard me on her local radio station, BBC W.M., when I was speaking with presenter Jenny Wilkes. Dora told me when she heard me mention my planned book of ladies' true wartime experiences, she knew she wanted to share her story with me. The following is Dora's story.

"Being born in Birmingham, I knew nothing about country life at all. I really was a city girl. I think it fair to say the only farm animals that I had seen were in school books, although I did have an uncle who kept a few racing pigeons, and I remember as a child in the late 1920's a story he told me of how in the Great War of 1914-18, they used pigeons to carry very important messages to France. My aunt used to say 'take no notice of him, young Dora. He'll tell you anything to make his blooming pigeons sound good'. I spent many happy days with my aunt and uncle, for my mother was a single parent, my father having died when I was only three years old. Mum told me that it was from lung damage that he suffered in the trenches in that Great War. He had also been badly wounded, and my uncle later told me that even when dad died he still carried bits of shrapnel in his body that the doctors had dare not remove, as some of it was to close to his heart.

It must have been very hard for mum, bringing me up alone, for I know now how hard she had to work as a factory hand, but she always put food on the table and kept me quite well dressed. If it had not been for my Aunt Gwen and Uncle Tom, though, I really would have been a latch key kid, for we always kept our front door key tied to the letter box with a piece of string, and when I got home from school I would just lift the latch and pull on the string to get the key and let myself in. This would have been when I was about ten years old, but until then I would call at my aunt's, and wait until mum picked me up once she finished work. Looking back, that key must have been on that piece of string for more then ten years to my knowledge, for it was still there when I left home at 19 years of age to join the Womens' Land Army. In all that time our home had been safe – not one intruder tried to break in, even though they could have just pulled on the string and let themselves in with the key, not that we really had anything of value to take, but the point I am trying to show is how honest people were then – I really think people cared so much more about one another. If you were daft enough to leave your key like that today you would soon have a burglar letting themselves in."

"On leaving school I started work for a shop selling ladies' clothes, and when I was put in the hat section, my mum would tell everyone 'oh, my daughter works in the millinery trade' so pleased was she that I had not gone into a factory. She always told me 'I don't want you following what I've had to do. You must set your sights higher'. I had to laugh one Sunday, though, when we attended church together.... an old lady who mum worked with, said to her on our way out of church, 'your Dora has grown up now. You must be very proud of her.' Mum replied, 'oh I am. she works so hard you know. She's in the millinery business, don't you know.' The dear old lady said, 'oh, how nice. That's what I would have liked to be, a missionary. You're right to be proud of her, she's doing God's work.' Well I had to laugh. It just knocked the wind out my mum. She didn't know what to say. I said 'come on mum, you don't have to keep singing my praises.' Mum said, 'I know the old girl's deaf but now she thinks you are a missionary.' I heard later that mum never did tell her what I really did for a living, so I dare say the dear old girl went all her life believing that I was a missionary."

"Well in 1940, much to mum's upset, I joined the Women's Land Army. I told her it was that or going into a munitions factory, and as she had always said 'you're not working in any factory', there wasn't much for her to say on the matter. I was now 19 years old and knew that I must do something to help my country, for so many of the other young men and women that I knew and worked with were now joining up to do their part for the war effort, that I had to do my bit. As I left the city to start my country life, of course mum was in tears, which upset me too. I asked my aunt and uncle to look after mum for me, and I put on a brave face as I entered the railway carriage. I pulled on the leather strap that lowered the carriage window, and waved to them until they were out of sight. As I went to sit down, there were two other girls dressed as I was in my new uniform. We soon got chatting, and like many others at that time became life-long friends from that day on. We had never left home before, so it really was a big adventure for us. It was a lovely day, and so good to see all the places that we had never seen before. We arrived at Cambridge station late in the afternoon, and were taken to a hostel for the night in a village I think was called Swavesey. We were told that we would only be staying for the night, as there was trouble on the lines just out of Cambridge, and as it would soon be repaired, we would carry on with our journey to Norwich tomorrow. Before we knew it we were called early in the morning and taken to the station and soon arrived at Norwich. To our surprise we were met by a horse and cart to take us to the farms we were to work on. What a treat it was for us city girls, for none of us had ever seen a horse let alone have a ride, with one pulling us along. Mr. Griggs was the man who met us, and in the weeks to come he was to teach us so much about farm animals and farming. I remember places such as Wymondham, Hethersett, Wramplingham, and of course Norwich, with great affection – such wonderful names the places had. The locals all laughed at me, though, because of my accent, but their's sounded just as strange to me. The first morning after breakfast I was asked to help with the milking. Now, as I have said, I'd never seen a real cow until now, and what a shock it all was to me. I must admit on first sight I was scared stiff of them, and stood there in fear when a voice bellowed out 'well don't jist look at 'em, girl – git milking 'em'. I didn't know where to start.... should I pump the tail to get the milk out or what?. I really had no idea at all what to do. The dairyman could see this and came over to me and said 'all right, don't get upset me love. I can show you what to do'. It was horrible, for just as I *did* start to get the hang of it, the cow went and kicked the bucket of milk all over me. I was crying and feeling very upset, and wanted my mum! Just as the dairyman was calming me down, still standing near to the cow, the blessed creature went and passed wind, and messed all over me! As bad as it was, once the dairyman started laughing, I couldn't help but laugh myself, and this turned my tears into those of laughter. The dairyman was also in tears now, because he was laughing so much. To this day I have never trusted cows, but I did go on to learn much about them. We girls were always told that it was the bull you have to watch out for, and you can imagine the dirty jokes we were told about them."

"I remember that before I left Norfolk, so many of the soldiers I saw at the Saturday night dances were being sent abroad to fight. I now know that many of these smashing lads died as prisoners of the Japanese in horrific circumstances. I only left Norfolk because my mother was taken very ill, and was asking for me. I still remember arriving home and, yes, the key was still on the piece of string. I let myself in and went straight up to her room, and said to her, 'I can't leave you on your own for a minute, can I, before you let yourself go?' I could see, though, that she was not at all well. I had been told she just had a bad chill, but this turned to pneumonia, and sadly I was to lose my dear mother. It hit me so hard, for she had cared so much for me, and although I still had my dear aunt and uncle, I now felt so alone in life. After all the funeral arrangements and sorting out what had to be done, I felt so ill myself, and was allowed to spend some time with my aunt and uncle. I think it fair to say it was their love that got me through at that time. When I returned to my Land Army duties I was sent down to Kent, as so many other girls had before me. I was still finding it so hard to get over my mother's death, then one day one of the girls working with me received word that her husband had been killed in action. It made me realise that her loss was far greater then mine, and it helped me to comfort her and do all I could to help her through it. Her husband had already been wounded in the disaster of Dunkirk, yet had come through it, only to be sent back into action to meet his death. As I had become close to her I was asked to drive her to Ashford station, for her to go home to her parents in London. I was never to see her again, although we kept in touch until the 1950s when I received a letter from her saying that she was going to marry her late husband's best mate, a chap called Dave Barrat, who had survived as a prisoner of the Japanese on the death railway. She told me it was to be a small do, at their local registry office, as she had already had one white wedding, for as you will know in those days it was not the done thing to have more than one white wedding – many people turned their noses up at her for even remarrying, but she seemed happy and told me that she and Dave were going to emigrate to Australia, as Dave had stopped off there on his way back to England after the war, and had fallen in love with that vast country. This was the last I was to hear of her, but I hope she had a good life, for I shall never forget the state she was in when I took her to the station that day."

"I spent the rest of the war on farms in and around Kent, and remember one farm I was at near Tenterden, where the people were so kind to us girls, and really appreciated what we were doing for our country. When it was harvest time it really was long days for us, sometimes starting at 6.00am and working through until 10.00pm. I remember, when the threshing machine came, none of us wanted to work with it, as it was so dusty and hard work. As hot water was so hard to come by, hot baths, something we girls dreamed of, were something of a luxury at this time, and at the farm at which I was staying, to get hot water we had to boil it in an old galvanized copper that Mrs. Jackson, the farmers wife, did her washing in, then by means of a bucket we took the water out of the copper and put it into the tin bath. As the water was so precious to us, we of course shared it – sometimes five of us to one lot of bath water. When I think of the colour it was when we had all finished, I think it fair to say that today I wouldn't even wash my dog in it.... oh, how times change."

"Once the harvest was all finished, one of the farmers put on a barn dance for us girls, and of course all the village folk from the surrounding area were invited. I remember one girl I knew at that time biked over fiftteen miles to get to it from where she was billeted, at a place called Goudhurst. Her name was Alice, and she had never ridden a bike before she joined the Land Army. I still laugh when I think of her on that bike, for she was all over the road – it's a good job the roads were not as busy as they are today or she wouldn't have lasted five minutes. I think I am right in saying that it was Mr. and Mrs. Joe Stubbings who put the barn dance on for us. I remember we all cleaned the barn out, and placed old beer boxes around the sides for people to sit on. There were three old boys who had served in the Great War, who brought their instruments to play to provide the music. One played a mouth organ, one a ukelele, and the other an old violin – or fiddle, as he called it. The other two old boys used to say, 'it's the right instrument for him love – he's a right fiddler, so watch him girls!' They really were so very good though, and I often smile to myself when I recall the scene to mind, for it was such a happy time, while all around us the world was going mad, killing one another, just so that one country could say they had more and were better than the other. Oh, how stupid mankind can be. Of course, most of our young men were away fighting for us, but we did have a few local air force chaps who came along. All of us girls would be looking for one of them to fall for us, for we outnumbered them by at least five to one. Mrs. Stubbings would make up a punch, but of course the air crew boys would slip in some alcohol when she wasn't looking and after a while we would all become merry and giggly. The whole village would be there, even the village bobby – he was the type who always felt he had to be in charge. For a policeman, I felt he was not really very tall.... I would have said only about 5ft 6inches at the most. He was also very fat, and we girls called him Mr. Bumble. Well he too got very merry as it was such a hot night and he kept drinking the punch. I heard him say to Mr. Stubbings, 'this is a very good punch that your Mrs. has made this year, Joe lad.' Well us young ones laughed, for we knew what was really in it. As the night went on Mr. Bumble drank more and more and soon became quite drunk. He was so hot that he took off his jacket and I can see him now with just his trousers and vest on, with his braces hanging down by his side – he really did look comical as he danced away. All of a sudden we heard an aeroplane overhead, its engine spluttering, and one of the air crew lads shouted out 'that's not one of ours, and by the sounds of it they're in trouble.' They had no sooner said this when the engine cut out altogether, and after a while we heard an almighty bang as the plane took the chimney stack clean off Mr. and Mrs. Stubbings' farmhouse. Mr. Bumble, who was well gone by this time, shouted 'come on lads, grab yourselves a pitch fork and let's get after him. Well the lads all grabbed a pitchfork from the side of the barn, and followed on behind Mr.Bumble, who of course had the biggest pitchfork of all. As he got to the barn door his trousers fell to his ankles and he fell over. What a sight we girls saw, for he had no underpants on, and his bare bum just sticking up in the air had us all in tears of laughter. The older ladies said 'turn away girls, it's not a sight for young girls to see'. Mr. Bumble picked himself up, and turned and gave us girls a very dirty look as he pulled his trousers back up. Of course by this time the rest of the lads had long gone, and Mr. Bumble, not wanting to miss out, set off after them. He was still staggering from the effect the punch was having on him but, wanting to be in charge, he was shouting at the top of his voice for the others to wait for him. It turned out to be a German plane that had crashed, and had come down in one of the fields nearby. The pilot had managed to bail out, and Mr. Bumble and the other men, who I must say were all half drunk, found him caught up in a tree hanging by his parachute. After they had cut him down they marched him back to the farm, prodding him in the back with their pitchforks. I tell you, whenever I watch Dad's Army on TV today, I can see how true to life it really was. We girls all rushed out to see him. He was only a young chap. Tall and slim, with lovely fair hair, and I suppose he was very frightened for his life. Mr. Bumble, who by now had started to sober up a little after all his running about, went off on his bike to get help from the army. As he biked away he shouted out 'lock him up somewhere safe, Joe'. Well, Mr.Stubbings did that all right – he locked him in the outside toilet, which stank to high heavens at the best of times. The evening came to an end after that, but I remember that in the morning when the army arrived back with Mr. Bumble, as they let this young German out of the old toilet, he was gasping in mouthfuls of fresh air. Mrs. Stubbings said 'poor kid, fancy keeping him in there all night', to which Mr. Stubbings replied, 'well, he had plenty of old newspaper to read'. You can guess what we used the old newspaper for – no soft toilet paper for us in those days. I think whenever I look back on my wartime memories, it is always this memory that stays with me, and I think after seeing Mr. Bumble's bare bum in the moonlight that evening in the barn doorway, we all agreed that we had given him the right name. Memories are such precious things that we can all cling to – good or bad, they are part of life. Now that I am old and blind, it is these wonderful memories of those days when I could see, and when I was so young and full of life, that help keep me going today. I was proud to help my country, and I think it turned a young naive girl into a woman, for I really had been to the University of Life."

"After the war, I returned home to Birmingham and met and married my husband Bob, who was in the R.A.F. during the war. He ended up in Hong Kong towards the end of the war, and saw the state of many of our dear soldiers who had been prisoners of the Japanese. When he told me of this he was in tears, and as he was not a man to cry easily, I know how alarming the sight of those brave lads must have been to him. I think he was helping to get them ready to come back home, but so many of them were just like walking skeletons, that it was a long time before they were well enough to travel. When Bob and I spoke of the war together, this was always his memory of it, so I know how lucky I was to have such amusing memories of my wartime days. As I have said, the saddest time for me was when I lost my dear mother, and seeing my friend so upset when she knew her husband had been killed in action."

"So, looking back over those dark years, I too was really one of the lucky ones, for so many families were just torn apart – fathers, sons, daughters and mothers died so that we could be free today. We must never forget them, and always wear our poppies with pride, as we show our respect for them every 11th November.... the 11th month, on the 11th day, on the 11th hour.... "WE WILL REMEMBER THEM".

Author's comments:
Dear Dora, Thank you for sharing your story with us. As you say, amusing at times, but with the war going on all around you I dare say you suffered many fearful moments. I, for one, agree with your final comments on remembrance and, as you say, we must never forget them. As one who has not known the suffering of war, in the two minute silence I always thank God for the ultimate sacrifice so many people made, so that I could have a life today. Thank you, Dora for the part you played in World War II, and for my life today. God Bless You.

Letters Section

Letter from Mrs. Andrea Hoyland, Boston, Lincolnshire.....

Dear Mr. Bentinck,

At the beginning of World War Two, I was only eight years of age and my brother nine, therefore it was our parents and their generation who had the active roles. A good family friend, Don Allan, now seventy five years of age, is still suffering the effects of torture and cruelty by the Japanese. He began his R.A.F. service as a rear gunner of a Lancaster bomber until he was sent out to Burma. Like many others he has written his book but like many others also, it was never published because there are so many similar accounts already on the shelves.

My late father, Norman Howard, also served in the R.A.F. but mainly because he was older, never left our shores to serve abroad. Firstly he worked on Barrage Balloon sites and when they were dispensed with, he serviced Lancaster and Wellington bombers at air fields all over the country. Though our air fields were under constant bombardment and many of his colleagues were maimed or killed, my father luckily survived with no more than shrapnel scars.

Having reached call-up age just two years before the war ended, my late husband, Kenneth Hoyland, joined the Royal Scots regiment. He served in Italy, Austria and finally Germany, where he was unfortunate to be among those relieving the concentration camps. Though I was never able to get him to speak freely about that experience, I know he was badly affected mentally by what he saw and had to do at the Belsen camp. Perhaps all this even contributed to his early death at the age of fifty four. In their own ways, heroes all, but there were others too, even on our streets at home.

In your interview on Radio Lincolnshire, you were looking for the ladies' side of WW2, so you may be interested in my Mother's escapades. Her name was Doris Howard but became known to everyone around at that time as Sargeant Major Howard. To my brother and I she was a stern but very loving person. Being a keen church goer, with a great interest in spiritualism, she always practised what was preached, so was the kindest, most helpful person, particularly in times of need.

At the beginning of the war, Mother began working as a tram conductress, helping to replace those called for service. Her tales of events were many, some tragic and some quite funny, like the evening of an air raid when the bombs started dropping soon after the siren. One blast had just missed the railway over Wicker Arches in Sheffield, but sliced the top deck off her tram and it landed several yards in front. Luckily all the passengers had alighted and run for shelter, so no one was hurt. Mother went through to her driver and found him frozen with fear. It was her instant remark which jolted him back to reality, "How many times have I told you not to slam the brake on so hard, just look what you've done now".

Yet her greatest efforts were when she joined the A.R.P. There her organising skills were well used training classes in first aid, showing how the gas mask was to be used, formed groups of fire watchers and instructed the use of stirrup pumps. Almost everyone was 'invited' to learn knitting, so hundreds of scarves, gloves, socks and balaclava helmets were made in Navy, Khaki and Air Force blue for the three services. Then when spirits were flagging, Mother would play the piano and lead community singing with her deep powerful contralto voice.

When the sirens wailed, Mother would rush into my room and in the darkness told me to dress quickly, while she opened the window. She then blew her whistle as she pulled on slacks, jumper, coat and tin hat. Incidentally, I still have that whistle and it works quite well. No one had a chance to sleep through a raid with the Sargeant Major on parade. Safely in our Anderson shelter with neighbours and friends, she was off to the A.R.P. station, where the head warden called a roll to make sure they were all present. Mother reckoned only half were there as most had forgotten false teeth, some had forgotten items of clothing and one turned up in his slippers – but none forgot their tin hats.

One dark night, when dashing out of our front gate to go on duty, she bumped into someone and stopped to apologise most profusely in the blackout. She then realised she was talking to the white painted band around the lamp post.

Even when the bombs were dropping every night, Mother would not agree to her children being evacuated to a safer place and told the authorities, "you have my husband, you're not taking the children as well". The Sheffield blitz was a harrowing time for all but it wasn't until the end of the war that we realised just how much our Mother had done. We knew of course that the wardens had to patrol the streets checking blackouts and getting people into shelters. What we didn't know was that the German planes, having dropped their bombs, then commenced to machine-gun down the roads, so Mother had to run along under cover of the hedges. She could never understand why they thought this would achieve anything and assumed they were using up ammunition or had learned how efficient our Home Guard and A.R.P. Wardens had become and were trying to eliminate them.

The incendiary bombs were a great worry as, apart from lighting up the whole town, they were the cause of so many losing their homes and businesses. It was surprising that, in comparison, so little damage was done to steel works and the railways. The easiest way to prevent fires starting was as our trained warden dealt with them – by using a stirrup pump or shovelling earth to douse them as they landed. Entering one garden to do just that when one landed quite close to a house, the owner quickly opened the door and shouted that she had dug up his onion patch. Without hesitation she replied, "make up your mind which you want – fried onions or the house burned down and PUT THAT LIGHT OUT". I'm told he made a formal complaint to her superiors, not just about his onions but the warden's 'uncaring attitude'. On another occasion a family ran from their home when an incendiary came down the chimney. No time to think about it, Mother ran in, scooped up the bomb on her shovel and brought it into the garden and doused it.

On patrol with two other wardens, they became aware of parachutes coming down over an old quarry site. One of the men thought the Germans were landing but the other remarked, "they wouldn't dare, not with Doris here. One command from her and they'll all surrender." They were not parachutists – just another fiendish device known to us as the Molotov cocktail which, upon landing, set off a spring device which sent out several bombs in different directions.

Then came the devastating land mines and Mother watched one land on a house at the end of a road and saw six others fall down in turn like a row of dominoes. Our home services were stretched to the limit and even as daylight came, everyone was helping to dig out survivors or the bodies of the less fortunate. Mother was among those who risked life and limb to bring out a tiny baby who was completely unharmed. Unfortunately the rest of the family were dead.

By now there were so many families left homeless and of course, Mother invited a large family to stay with us. Regretably, the thanks of this family didn't stretch to helping with household chores or cooking and they even sat around waiting for Mother to come in from work to cook a meal for all. That is, until she put her foot down. After sitting awhile writing, she rose to announce she had prepared some house rules which must be followed, "or find somewhere else to idle around".

Our next house guests were two soldiers billeted with us after being evacuated from Dunkirk. For the few days they were with us there were no problems at all, probably because they were under orders to be helpful. Some time later, Mother received two very nice thank-you letters from them.

I often think of Mother when I watch an episode of "Dad's Army" on television, as one sunny day she was on phone duty in the warden's station at our local school, standing by the open window watching our Home Guard assemble in the yard. As these middle-aged-to-older men stood around talking in groups, she became aware of an irresistable urge to which she finally gave way. Shouting commands to them, they lined up and she drilled and marched them up and down the yard. It was quite some time before they realised their officer wasn't present at which point she moved away from the window so they wouldn't know who had given the orders.

When it was all over and the men were coming home, one of them told Mother they could have done with people like her in the services. Her reply to that comment was, "well at least you got leave from time to time, while we at home were on duty five years without a break".

When my parents retired in 1968, my husband and I had already moved to Boston in Lincolnshire and Mother was overjoyed to come here and spend her last years in the county where she was born. Until she died in 1977, she continued to help and entertain, supported charities and organised social events, whist drives and bingo for her fellow senior citizens. In short, she spent her life being a good Christian and made many new friends here. Therefore we should not have been surprised when we took her to church for that very last time and found the place packed with people. When we raised our voices in song for her very favourite hymn, I could have sworn I heard that wonderful rich contralto voice above all others, singing "Abide With Me".

Even though she was our Mother, I have to admit the title of her obituary notice in the Sheffield paper, "Guardian Angel in a Tin Hat" was most appropriate. There was a similar piece in the Lincolnshire papers but it referred more to her later life. I have enclosed a cutting from the paper as it has her photo. You need not return it if you wish to keep it as I have others.

Hoping all this will be of some interest to you.

Yours sincerely,

Mrs. A. Hoyland.

Letter from Miss Joan Clark, The Wirral, Merseyside.....

Dear Michael,

I have read your other books and have found them of great interest. I really thought that I knew what our brave Far Eastern Prisoners of War went through, but reading your books has shown me that I knew nothing of what they really gave for my today.

As you say, Michael, they really are such heroes, and we owe them so very much for what they gave and suffered for us to be here today.

In the Second World War I was a Land Army girl, and until then I had never left my dear old Liverpool. My boyfriend was from Cambridge, and I met him in Liverpool just a few days before he and his chums sailed for the Far East, although at that time we didn't know this was to be their destination. As I say, I only knew him for a short time, after we met at a dance in Liverpool. I shall never forget the day he set sail from Liverpool – it was a grey October day in 1941, and I was in tears. I begged him to take care and keep safe, but alas it was not to be, for he died from cholera while a prisoner of the Japanese, on that notorious death railway, and I am sure you will have heard much more than I about that gruesome death. For me, in the 1940s, it was a very exciting time, for I was sent to a farm in Suffolk with two other girls, Peggy and Doris. We were all scared stiff as we had never left home before, and I can still remember crying on the journey wondering what was to become of us. We arrived at the farm in the evening and the owners, Mr. and Mrs. Ambrose, were there to greet us. Mrs. Ambrose had cooked us a home-made steak and kidney pie, and she made us feel so at home. Mr. Ambrose sat smoking his pipe in the corner of the room in his large armchair while us girls had our dinner, and once we had finished he said, "well girls, I thinks you best git to bed now. We have an early start here every morning". We were taken to our room, which all three of us had to share. Doris and I shared a double bed, and Peggy had a small camp bed at the end of ours. We lay in bed and chatted about our home life, and we got to know a little about one another. It turned out that Peggy's boyfriend had also gone off to fight, with my boyfriend John, but Doris told us that she did not have any boyfriends, as her mother had told her that boys only wanted girls for one thing, and I think this had scared her off men. The next morning at 6.00am we were awoken by a bang on the door and told to be down for breakfast in half an hour. It really was a smashing cooked breakfast, Mr. Ambrose said "this will set you up for the day girls". As we sat eating our breakfast a smashing young lad came into the room, and we all stared at him. Mr. Ambrose said, "say hello to your new workmates then Jack lad". He nodded to us and muttered "morning". We said "hello" back but all felt so silly in our overalls and boots – not very lady-like I can assure you.

Over the next year I learnt all I could about farming, and about life. And, yes, I fell in love with Jack. I think Peggy and Doris both wished he had wanted them, but he made it really clear that I was the one he had eyes for. His father would do all he could to keep us apart but we always found some way to be together. I am sure that you will know what the power of love can do. I would sneak out at night and meet him in the barn, in the hay loft, and one night after doing what lovers do we fell asleep in each others arms. When we awoke in the morning there stood Mr. Ambrose, who never spared my blushes at all. I was soon moved off to another farm, and Jack joined the army. I learnt some time after that he had been killed in action. War is a terrible thing, Michael, for it breaks the hearts of ordinary people. It is the political men that start them, but the ordinary people that have to fight and suffer in them and, as you know, so many lives are wrecked because of them.

One thing I will never forget is seeing those poor lads who came home from the Far East in late 1945. I was at the Liverpool docks to greet them, and it was just like watching walking skeletons coming ashore. Those poor boys were so very thin, most of them having lost half their body weight. I could see then that they would need a lot of help to get back to a normal life again but, as we now know, for so many of them life would never be normal again.

Michael, as for me I never married, for I could never meet anyone to replace my love for Jack. I also never forgot those days of love in the hay loft, for Jack was the only man I shared my love with in that way, and I believe that I was the only girl he had ever known in this way. I know it was a very special time for us. Yes, a very precious time in our lives, when there was the nightmare of war all around us, and to this day I never regret my time as a Land Army girl, for it brought me to my darling Jack.

In my life I have often laughed at people who think I know nothing of love and life just because I am a Miss, but Michael, as you can see, I have known what the power of love can bring to one's life. It was some years before I heard about John, and of how he died, for as I said I only knew him for a short time, but I know that like Jack he was a real man and I could never meet anyone to match them, and so I decided to stay single. I don't think there is a day that goes by when I don't think of them, and I know if they had not answered the call of King and country, then none of us would enjoy the life that we have today. I thank you so much, Michael, for all you and your dear wife do for us old timers, and thanks to you I know that those of us who lived through World War II will never be forgotten. I would ask you to keep up your writing and tell the world what we owe to men like John and Jack.

Yours faithfully,
Miss Joan Clark.

Letter from Mrs. E. Knight, Upton, Wirral.....

Dear Mr. Bentinck,

I was pleased to hear you speaking on our local BBC Merseyside, with Linda McDermott when you mentioned you were writing a new book on ladies' stories of World War II. I am so glad that someone cares enough about us old ladies to want to write our stories.

I joined the Women's Land Army, and soon after I was sent

instructions to travel to St Erth in Cornwall. I had been given the name of another girl who was to travel with me, Beattie, and we were to become the greatest of friends.

It was an August day – Bank Holiday Monday – and the crowds on the train had been celebrating, so we were given quite a lot of hassel over our brand new uniforms. We really stood out like a couple of sore thumbs. We survived the journey though, all 14 hours of it, and I can still remember the tea we had in jam jars on Plymouth station, for in those days we couldn't afford flasks.

When we arrived at the country station of St Erth, we were met and taken to our farm, or should I say our dump. One of the other Land Army girls showed us where we would be sleeping – it was just a converted hen house.... the only difference was that we were now to be the hens! We shared this hen house with ten other girls. It consisted of six double wooden bunk beds, the pillow cases were filled with straw, and we had large army grey blankets. Washing facilities consisted of two old washstands that the basins were built into, with two large jugs of cold water, which we got from a well outside. At least there was a pump over the well to pump the water up. The doorway was only four feet high and covered by heavy sacking. The food we were given was just dreadful. I can remember some of us deciding to try for a lift to Penzance to buy food, and an army supply truck was our salvation. The soldiers who were in the back of the lorry gave us boxes of jam tarts, which were the best things we had eaten since we left home – until then we had mainly been given saffron bread.

We decided to apply for a transfer, and my friend and I had decided to try and stick together. Life wasn't what we had expected at all, but soon we were transferred to Gunnislake to do dairy work. It was out of the frying pan into the fire, for our home was now an old nissen hut and the dairy an old corrugated shed. I was given the job of washing the milk bottles and crates – all by hand of course. My friend had to go with the boss to deliver the milk door to door. I can remember being told off for not stirring the churns of milk before I had filled the bottles, so the customers either had pure cream, or the unlucky ones had skimmed milk. After a while we realised that no one in the village ever spoke to us, and we were treated like foreigners. We wondered if it was our breeches and dungarees, which made us look of such a low standing, but this was our uniform – we had that or nothing at all.

After a while we realised that our boss was also a peeping tom, so once again our bags were packed and another transfer applied for. This time we headed for Liskeard. If we thought Tavistock had been rough, this was far worse. We were on a farm right on the top of a hill near Seaton, and about a mile walk up an old hill track from the main road. We were employed here as general farm workers – up at the crack of dawn, then bring the cows in and wash and milk them. Only when all this work was done could we eat. No one spoke at table, and the farmer's wife and us two girls, as soon as we had finished our food and tidied up had to go straight back to work, driving tractors, carrying hay for the horses, plus all the general farm work we had to do. One morning after breakfast, the farmer said to me, "you, madam, can go to the bottom field where you will find a dead sheep. I want you to pull all of the wool off of it, then put the sheep in this sack and bury it and make sure that you bury it deep, in case the dogs and foxes get smell of it". Did my heart sink – I thought he must be kidding me. But alas he was not, and I was soon told to go and get on with it. I set off with the sacks and a spade, and soon found the sheep. The easy part was pulling the wool out of it, the hard work was digging a grave for it. I had been told many times that we were digging for victory, but this time I couldn't see what part I was really playing in the war effort. I dug the grave as deep as I could and dragged the dead sheep into it. As it fell in, it landed on its back, with four very stiff legs sticking up in the air. The trouble was, parts of the legs were sticking out of the top of the grave. What was I going to do? I had the spade by me and a sack full of wool, and I knew if I didn't get back to the farm soon then I would be in trouble, because I knew that there would be many more jobs lined up for me to do. So I took the spade and broke the legs off the dead sheep, then quickly covered the earth over it. I hated myself then, and to this day I still feel bad about what I did to the poor dead creature.

Our only amusement consisted of the twice-weekly local village hop, after which, when we arrived back at the farm, the farmer always knew just who we had spoken to, and what about. He always gloated on how he was having us watched, even when we used to go into the village for gallons of paraffin for the tractor – two gallons each we had to carry back up that old hill track. Yes, he tried demeaning us in every way he could, but when he tried the wandering hands game on me, with my hands full with buckets of fresh milk, he picked on the wrong girl, for I drenched him with both buckets. I often wonder what his wife had to say to him about it, but knowing him he would bluff his way out of it.

Once again our bags were soon packed – we never even had breakfast that day, we just did a runner down the hill. It was 7.30 in the morning and we were two stoney broke girls. Luck was with us though, and a gentleman asked us where we were going so early in the morning. We told him our story, and he turned out to be our knight in shining armour. He was a retired ships captain, and he took us to his bungalow, where he gave us a good breakfast and arranged bed and breakfast accommodation for us. The next morning we were taken to the rectory at St. Germans and given a warrant to travel to Penzance to catch a ferry to the Scilly Isles. I think we were the only girls from Cheshire who ever travelled so far in our so called dig for victory.

Life was much easier now – we boarded with a family who really had very little themselves but were so very kind to us. When I think of the primative conditions that we all lived in! There was only one flush toilet on the island, owned by Mrs. Chudliegh. We girls loved to work near her house because she would allow us to use this wonderful flush toilet. It was wonderful not to have to use a bucket, or go behind the bushes, like we had to at our digs, or wherever we were working. We may have been poor back home in Birkenhead, but we did have a flush toilet, and a bathroom! I never did have a bath at these farms we stayed at, so the only time I did so was when I got home on leave, which was on two warrants a year, or if my parents sent me the money for the fare.

Being with girls on market gardening work, life was good for us. We planted potatoes and tomatoes, and harvested them when they were ready. Our foreman, Mr. Collins, was so very kind to us all – he was a real gentleman. He used to drive the plough, and we followed behind planting and picking whatever we were working on at that time. If we decided we needed a break (it was back-breaking work, walking in the furrows) we would give a long steady whistle and the shire horse would stop, and we had a five minute breather before Mr. Collins could get dear old Dobbin to move on again. Mr. Collins was the only one to invite us all to tea at his family home. What a treat it was, and his family were all so very interested to hear where we lived –

it seemed like another world to them, we also met many people who had never left the island in their lives. All newspapers, clothes, and food etc, had to be brought from Penzance by steamer which only came every other day. There was one telephone box which hardly ever worked. The radio was powered by an old accumulator which we could not always get charged, so we had to go without the radio news. Our meeting place when not at work was the post office-cum-general stores-cum-pub. We would meet up here with the other girls whenever we could. I can remember some sailors coming ashore and we were all singing and enjoying ourselves. I personally thought I was Deanna Durbin, and sang 'I can see the lights of home', during which there was a deadly hush until I finished, then there would be a lot of bluster to cover up all the girls' emotions. At the weekends we would catch a fishing boat to St. Mary, the largest island, and would have to spend the night here and catch the boat back next morning. We were able to see more of life on these weekend visits, and buy a newspaper, and sometimes some sweets, but the highlight of the weekend was always our Saturday night dance at the town hall. We had very few civvy clothes as we had to use our clothing coupons for our Land Army uniforms etc, so with our clean pressed dungarees, we hit the dance floor. It was such good fun that we would dance every dance – no sitting out for us. We met people from all walks of life at these times, not just farmers who we saw day in day out, and it was so good to have conversations of real interest with these people. In many ways we were so isolated for we had no books to read and no library to go to, and we weren't really accepted in the NAAFI and canteens, but I must say that forces personnel were always kind to us, and considerate whenever we travelled on trains, always helping us with our bags – maybe it was our scouse accent that they liked. Looking back I suppose it is always the good things one likes to remember and for me those Saturday night dances were just great.

The locals told us one day that a young sailor from Birkenhead was buried in the local churchyard so we collected as much detail as we could and found that Beattie, my friend, lived quite near to his home, so she called to say that we had visited his grave and that it was being looked after by the local people. We were on Christmas leave at this time, and on the day of our return journey, the sailor's family sent us a holly wreath for us to place on his grave for them. It was tied to our case and arrived at Tresco somewhat bedraggled, its long journey had taken all the berries off of it, but we did our bit and laid it on the young sailor's grave for his family, for he really had paid the price like so many others for King and country.

Soon after this we were moved again. I can't recall why but we were transferred to Penzance, but on arrival were sent to Hearmoor about two miles outside of town, where we were billeted at the local hairdressers. Our work now was picking sprouts, peas and cauliflowers, which were sent up to London by train. Picking sprouts with frost on them was not a pleasant job at all – our fingers were more like frozen sausages, and our feet just like blocks of ice. I think the worst job for us was the cauliflowers, as we had to walk between the rows, the men cutting them off their stalks, and cutting the long leaves off of them, and us picking them up and throwing them into large skips which, when full, we had to carry on our backs. These skips were about 4 feet high by 3 feet in diameter, and would hold about twenty good size caulies. Once our skip was full we would walk to the end of the row, and empty them out where the boss man packed them neatly into crates ready to go off to market. The sprouts we put into green net bags.

Another job I can well remember doing was picking violets and we also did this on frosty mornings. Now I hate violets, the poor innocent flower. It caused so much misery and discomfort – after all, you couldn't eat them, and when we were very hungry we used to eat the raw vegetables to keep us going, as we never received much food back at our digs.

When working we had a morning break which we called elevenses, but the locals called croust, when we would go together down to the farmyard sheds. The bosses went into the packing shed for their croust, and when they had eaten and drunk their fill, they called us girls to eat and drink anything that was left – after all, we were their labourers. As our landlady never gave us any croust, Beattie and I were always hungry and always glad of the cakes and sandwiches that we got at this time of the day. As our living accomodation was not too good we asked again for a move, and we were transferred into a hostel just outside Penzance – today it is a helicopter pad. At last we had hot water and warm rooms, proper meals, good beds, and lots of other girls to mix with.... and lots of laughs at last! We also had a warden to look out for us and make sure we were cared for. It really was wonderful for us, and to have the use of a flushing toilet was a real treat, for every day at work the hedgerow became the toilet for us Land Army girls. One day at work I was answering a call of nature down in a ditch behind a hedgerow when I got the shock of my life; all of a sudden I heard American mens' voices calling out "Up one two three four!" I nearly died on the spot, but as these American soldiers came marching by, thank goodness their officer shouted out the order to keep eyes front – it did spare my blushes a little. Thank goodness our paths never crossed again, but when I think of American soldiers it is always that situation that comes to mind, and yes, it still makes me blush. I also remember the night we went to a dance on the promenade at the pavilion, only to find that we were 2 pence short of our entrance fee. We couldn't go back to the hostel, not after we had come all this way for our night out, and of course we were all excited and looking forward to a good night of dancing, so we chatted to a group of sailors who were also waiting to go in, and thankfully they took pity on us and gave us the money we needed. We never did see them again after that and we often wondered if they survived the war, for as you know, so many of our ships went down and so many of those wonderful young men found a watery grave. I will never forget their good turn to us that evening, and I hope and pray that they went on to have a full and happy life.

We were still working at Heamoor Farm and the job this particular day was to pull up leeks. We now had bikes to get around on – Land Army issue of course – but it made our three mile trip better for us than having to walk to work each day. On this day it was raining slightly as we set off, and we had our macs, souwesters and leggings etc. to help keep us warm and dry. One of our bikes got a puncture so we dropped it off at the village garage, where one of the men was kind enough to repair it. We then walked the rest of the way to work, or gave the girl without a bike a lift on one of ours by one of us standing up and peddling while she sat on the seat with her legs stretched out to the sides. We worked steadily that day from 8.00am and were told we would finish that evening about 7.00pm. By the time it was time for our morning croust, we were all soaking wet, and knew that we still had a long day ahead of us. The boss kept coming to check on us, and told us not to worry as we could all have a hot bath that night back at the hostel. This was no consolation to us as by 3.00pm that afternoon Beattie and I were like a couple of drowned rats, and were feeling so cold and unwell because of it, that we decided enough was enough, and as we still had to bike the 3 miles back to the hostel, we were going now – whatever the boss said.

Once back at the hostel the warden ran us hot baths, and told us, "you two girls are so silly. You should have come back much sooner. The other girls all came back at midday, and I wondered why you weren't with them". So we told her what a slave driver our boss was. I don't think it did much good though, for it was always hard work for us on the farm.

About this time I was also suffering from a recurring abcess at the base of my spine. The chemist I explained my problem to said that if it didn't clear up soon, then I would need an operation, so plans had to be made about returning home for me. If you didn't work you didn't get paid, and as I was in so much pain my parents insisted that I come home to be properly cared for. It became a hospital job, with stays of three weeks on two occasions. Once I was completely better I returned to work, but this time nearer to home. I can remember being in the fields when V.E. Day arrived, for even if at last we dare believe that the war would soon be over, there was still plenty of work to be done to make our country great again. We had plenty of hugs and cheers on that day I can tell you, but the produce had to be ready for market next morning so there was no slacking for us. We did have Irish labourers working with us now and they did all the heavy lifting for us, which I really did appreciate after my back operation. Soon after this time I decided that I had now done enough digging for victory, and decided to call it a day. I returned my uniforms, and received my papers which stated I was now released.

I was able to buy some clothing coupons on the black market, to buy some civilian clothes, as the official office had refused me any. I was drafted into a munitions factory in Chester, using a works bus for transport, and worked a three shift system, but that's another story, and as you know, I am telling you of my Land Army days.

We took men's places and did a man's job in World War II, and have been overlooked for years. Our badge had a crown on it, we came under the Ministry of Agriculture and Fisheries admin, yet we were soon forgotten.

I wish you good luck in all you do with your efforts to help us older ones who did their bit in the dig for "Victory". I look forward to reading your new publication, and thank you for flying the flag for us proud Land Army Girls.

Yours thankfully,

Ellen Knight.

P.S. At the start of the war I had applied to join the A.T.S. but after their medical I was refused with suspected signs of T.B. I went on to join the Land Army on my 18th Birthday in 1942, and left home six weeks later. Perhaps all that fresh air helped my lungs but I don't think being wet through so many times did me much good. This year I went back to the Scilly Isles, at 73 years of age, and stood and relived all those times that Beattie and I had spent there, and although the place had changed so very much, my memories of it are still as if it was yesterday.

Letter from Mrs. Jessie Hicks, St. Austell, Cornwall.....

Dear Mr. Bentinck,

I too was a Land Army girl, as I know my sister Mrs. Margaret Senior of Sheffield, has written to tell you. The following is an account of just a little of my time in the Women's Land Army.

How I joined the Land Army was a funny thing really – my friend at work asked me if I would go with her for moral support, as she was going to join. So off I went with her to the recruiting centre in Sheffield, which, to cut the story short, resulted in me joining and her backing out.

It was 1943, and I was just a young teenager, but I remember getting on the train very early one morning at Sheffield station, and after a very long and tiring day of travelling, I arrived at St. Erth in Cornwall very late in the evening. It was like a foreign country – I couldn't understand the Cornish dialect, and they certainly couldn't understand me. I do remember the peace and quiet after the terrible air raids that had been inflicted on Sheffield.

I was told I would be here for a month to learn the 101 jobs that farming entails. One memory is having to learn to milk, on a nearly dry cow. Once trained we were all sent our different ways to work on the farms where we were needed. I did general farm work, rising very early in the morning to do the hand milking, all before breakfast, then after breakfast it was the mucking out and washing out. Thank goodness it was done this way round, for I don't think I could have eaten much after mucking out. Once this was done the day's work really started, for whatever season it was, it was always hard work. It ranged from planting potatoes to lifting them, hoeing turnips and mangels, faring the hedges, and harvesting the corn, when it was double summer time, for the days were so long it seemed that as soon as I finally got to bed, it was time to get up again. You will have heard the saying 'make hay while the sun shines', well we had to make hay while the moon shone as well. I remember having to take one of the carthorses to the blacksmiths to be re-shoed, a distance of 4 miles through a maze of Cornish country lanes; what a nightmare it was, there being no signposts to tell me the way.

It really was hard work, and I think the most I ever earned was 24 shillings a week. However, things really improved for me when the farm I was on had one of the first ever milking parlours installed.

After the war I decided to leave the Land Army, in 1946. I was undecided whether to stay in Cornwall or to go back to Sheffield, but my husband-to-be was demobbed, after 6 years in the R.A.F. since 1940, and came back to his home at Lostwithiel. We met, and married 8 months later, so I was to stay in Cornwall, and today my husband and I are still so very happy together and, yes, I can now understand the Cornish dialect, for as you can see, all those years ago when I arrived at St. Erth, it was to become my home and my life.

Best wishes,

Mrs. Jessie Hicks.

Overleaf is an article featuring Ken and Jessie Hicks, written by Richard Price of the Western Morning News, as part of their series covering those couples celebrating their Golden Wedding Anniversary.....

LOVE came around in the nick of time for Ken and Jessie Hicks – they met as Jessie celebrated her last night in the West Country at a dance in Lostwithiel.

"Then Ken came along and persuaded me to stay. We have been together ever since," she says.

It was 1946 and Ken had just been demobbed from the R.A.F., while Jessie was set to return to Sheffield after a spell in the Land Army. Eight whirlwind months later – on May 14, 1947 they were married, settling in the Lostwithiel area.

In 1948 their first son, Christopher, was born and they moved to Sheffield. But they were back within two years. "The way I see it, why live anywhere else when you can live in Cornwall?" said Jessie, 70.

Second son Peter came along in 1952 and for many years they worked long hours on the land to provide a happy home for their family.

"It was hard work for us in those days, much harder than people have it these days, but we have always had each other," said Ken, 74. "We have always been able to work through our problems together."

Eventually they decided to move into Lostwithiel itself, where Ken went to work in the milk factory. During this time they moved to Mill Gardens, where Jessie took on the job of warden in the flats for the elderly.

Family has always been their number one concern. This came to the fore when they took in their baby granddaughter Sarah, who had to be parted from son Peter because of family circumstances.

They cared for her until she was five, when she was able to return to her father. Throughout the years that followed they remained close to the girl they loved as their own daughter.

But in August 1994, Ken and Jessie were devastated by Sarah's tragic death in a road accident when she was 16. Throughout those difficult times it was their love for each other and their family which kept them going.

"We still miss her terribly and we have had some very hard times," Ken said. "But we also have so much to be happy about."

They have two young nieces and a 17-year-old grandson, David, of whom they are tremendously proud.

"He has a place at Exeter University to read law, so it looks like his life will be slightly different to ours!" Ken said.

Christopher Hicks, who nominated his parents for the award with his wife Sheila, said: "We know how special they are to us and how special they were to our niece."

Letter from Mrs D. Kurjan, Preston, Lancs.....

Dear Mr Bentinck,
I was most interested to read your article regarding land girls. Oddly enough, the happiest memories for me were the War years. Sad for some, happy for me. It all started one day when my father brought a lady and her two children to our house. The mother and her children were evacuees from London, which at that time was being bombed daily. My father explained that they were going to live with us, and they soon got married. I had been very close to my father; we went on long walks and bicycle rides, went to the cinema and to football matches. Having lost my mother as a child, my father and I went nearly everywhere together.

After the wedding, all this stopped. My stepmother and stepsisters took over, so I thought. They shared my room, my clothes, and my bicycle. You can tell how spoilt and selfish I was. So one day I thought "I've had enough of this. I'm going to take myself off". I got an application form, filled it in, and had a medical for the Women's Land Army, which I passed.

The day came when I got a travel warrant and instructions as to where I should go. It was to Lazenby, in Cumberland – a beautiful place with lovely scenery and a river. I've never seen anywhere so lovely.

Some of the girls went to different farms and some, like me, went into hostels. I arrived at the hostel and was taken to the office of the warden, Mrs Odell, who welcomed me with tea and biscuits, told me the rules, and then showed me round the hostel. There was a recreation room, showers, a dining room and a dormitory with bunk beds down each side of the room. The beds had an upper and lower bunk with mattresses as hard as rock, but we got used to them eventually. The warden gave me my uniform – light brown overalls, yellow shirts and green v-neck jumpers for outside work. On duty we had brown floppy hats, and for off-duty times, a lovely fitted brown jacket, a sort of riding pants, and a green beret.

Later the other girls came home from the fields, went to the showers and then came in for a meal. I was introduced to them, about 30 in all. We all got up early the next morning and waited outside for the Land Army lorries, taking us, in gangs, to the farms.

Sometimes, we worked for weeks on the same farm, and when the work was finished we went on to another farm. In winter we worked in a shed, chopping up wood. The work was hard but we had help. We worked with displaced persons and prisoners of war – Germans, Italians, Estonians and more. The Germans were hard workers but the Italians hated going to work in the rain, although they were very romantic! The Germans used to do a lot of heavy lifting for us, so in return for this, we used to get them cigarettes at the village shop, which sold nearly everything. The owners had lost someone in the war and would not sell the prisoners cigarettes or anything else.

For anyone who wanted to go home, free railway passes were given at the weekend. So we had an early lunch on Saturday. If you stayed, the warden served some sort of sponge cake with custard. If you wanted to take it with you, she always joked, saying to the Lancashire girls, "do you want it now or in your hand", without pronouncing the 'h', in a most preposterous Lancashire accent.

The farmers used to sell us large pieces of bacon, eggs, cheese and butter, which was a godsend with all the rationing, with 2oz of this and 2oz of that. I went home at weekends with all these good things, and I wore my jacket and beret – I really thought I was something. My father, stepmother and stepsisters were always pleased to see me and pleased with what I had taken home to them.

Back at the hostel things went on as normal, until one day in the dining room Mrs Odell, with her eagle eyes, noticed one girl with a bigger appetite than usual, and I heard her say "I'll have her in for a medical". The next day, they said she wasn't well, so would not be repor-ting for work. When we got back in the evening, she and all her belongings had gone. We all looked at each other in a knowing way, because we all knew she was pregnant, but none of us said anything.

It wasn't all hard work and we had some lovely times. We went in the lorries two evenings a week to Penrith, to dances at the Drill Hall, as there were only two picture places. We also had dances at the hostel to which the displaced persons were invited. If we did not go home at the weekend we sometimes went to Carlisle, which was a bit like Blackburn, the town where I was born. Both had a C & A, and a Woolworth's, only Blackburn had more breweries. Near Blackburn town centre Thwaites, Mercer, Lion and Duttons all had breweries, and in the centre of those thriving breweries was a Salvation Army church with big lettering on the walls saying 'Down with drink'. Yet all the

'Sally' army girls went into the pubs selling the War Cry newspapers to raise money for the cause of abolishing the 'demon drink'.

Going back to those evenings out with the lorries, on the way home we would always sing. The Lancashire girls sang 'She's a lassie from Lancashire' and the Geordie girls sang 'The Bladen Races'. Each sang songs from where they came from – it was a happy time.

We had a cook at the hostel who was a displaced person. He was an Austrian called Emile. Besides cooking he used to stoke up the boiler at the back of the hostel where there were lots of cinders which had been raked out. The reason I am telling you about this is because a lady used to come in daily to clean and wash the dishes and one day Emile and the lady came to the warden to give notice that they were leaving, and were going to get married and work as a cook and housekeeper somewhere. Mrs Odell asked Jenny, the lady, "where ever did you do your courting?" to which Jenny replied "amongst the cinders". I had to laugh. I was sorry they were going because Emile had been very kind to me and helpful. He used to offer me his breakfast when it was bacon or pork sausages as he never ate pork. But I always refused because I didn't want the girls to think I was being favoured. The reason they gave notice was because, to our great sadness, the Land Army was being disbanded and we all knew we would be soon going home.

I suppose you are thinking there was no romance in my life. You would be wrong. After we disbanded I married one of those displaced persons, a Polish man named Jozef. We had and I still have four children, who I love dearly. Sadly my husband died young, when my youngest was only 3 years old.

So, you see, my happiest, carefree years, were with the Land Army.

Yours sincerely,

Mrs D. Kurjan.

Letter from Mrs. N. Farrow, Stow-on-the-Wold, Cheltenham.....

Dear Mr. Bentinck,

I was lucky today to hear your programme on BBC Hereford and Worcester, with Mark Develin, and was very interested in your stories of World War II. When I heard you say how you would be interested to hear from ladies who did their bit in the war for King and country I thought "yes, I was one of those", and so I have put pen to paper, to tell you just a little of my life at that time.

I was 20 years old when war broke out, and was working in a very large house for a lady whose husband had been the head of the orange men in Ireland. In the 1920s uprising they had to flee Ireland. Their daughter had joined the Black Shirt movement, and Sir Oswald Mosely, and the Milford Girls, and William Joyce, were frequent visitors. I had to get out for I knew it was not good for me to be associated with any of this, so I left to join the Women's Land Army. Once I had registered I was sent to a farm to start my work in our dig for victory. Here I was, me who had washed precious china and silver, now having to wash large churns and separators with my bare hands, in all weathers.... oh, how my poor hands suffered. I had to fill a large copper, and light it, as there was no running water, only water from the farm well, so of course to get hot water it had to be boiled in this copper. The floor of the dairy consisted of flagstones, which made your feet like blocks of ice in the winter. There was a stallion on the farm and I had to pass by his stable each morning to get to feed the chickens and collect the eggs. I used to tiptoe by his stable, and he used to kick out at the stable door and walls, which terrified me.

After a year I had been through enough, especially when the farmer got fresh with me. Although he never molested me in any way, his remarks and his trying to touch me was enough to warn me that it was time to move on. I went back to the Land Army board to ask if I could join the forces, but they told me I was now in a reserved occupation, but I could move over to munitions for a while, in a factory. At this time the Army Farms Depot at Wandworth was bombed, and it was hastily converted into a three story factory; it had been a stick mill years before. Anyway, I got a job packing forms for various units around the country. I worked here from 7.30am until 6.00pm, seven days a week, under very difficult conditions, especially in the winter time, for

I had to cycle 10 miles every night and morning, and in really bad weather I would have to walk it. There were seven of us living at home at this time, and I can still remember my mother making up our sandwiches for our packed lunches. By the way, there were fourteen of us at home usually until the war came along – 12 girls and two boys, plus mum and dad. My father was a builder, and as he did not earn much, I know what a struggle it must have been to keep us all fed and clothed, hence we frequently had dripping or just beetroot in our sandwiches for lunch, and cocoa without sugar to wash them down. I joined the Red Cross, and after returning home from work just before 7.00pm, I would change into my uniform and go off to do my duty, especially if there was an alert on, when we would stay out all night. Then it would be straight off to work next morning. How I managed to stay awake is a miracle. We also did hospital duty at weekends, which entailed doing all the dirty work like emptying the bed pans and giving the patients bed baths, but as you can imagine, those poor nurses were kept so busy it was a pleasure to be of help to them, for their job is hard at the best of times, but in war time it's much worse for them.

Two of my sisters worked in the aircraft factories, one of them helping to make gliders for the invasion to come. At the depot where I worked I was put in charge of first aid, and had a few panicks. Once, when one girl stabbed an artery in her arm, blood was everywhere but I managed to stop it with a coin wrapped in a hanky and I bandaged it up tightly, before sending her off to hospital. I treated broken limbs, and even helped deliver babies when they wanted to get into the world in a hurry. Now and again we held dances in the village halls, and soldiers of all nationalities came for an evening out. It was at this time that I met my husband-to-be, a policeman in the dog patrol section, who was stationed at the local aerodrome. I was rushed into hospital with appendicitis, and the man who was to be my husband came to see my father to ask if he could borrow his guns. He also brought my mother to visit me in hospital. I nearly fell out of the bed when this young airman came in with my mum. To cut a long story short, we had our Golden Wedding in September 1996. We have three children, four grandchildren plus two great-grandchildren. So thanks to the war I met my dear husband.

Before I close, I do remember that one farm I was at was badly bombed, killing the bull, and horses, plus the pigs and sheep. Luckily they missed the house where we were all trying to sleep, but it did blow all the windows out and took all the tiles off the roof. I remember there was a large searchlight on the edge of the village, and that when the planes left Bristol after their bombing raids, the ack-ack was just deafening. We also had an American camp near to us at this time.... my, what a fast lot they were. Talk about overpaid, over-sexed, and over here – that was them alright. But to be honest, they were very generous with cigarettes, chewing gum, and tins of fruit etc, for everything was on ration, and to have a tin of fruit for sweet with your meal was a godsend. Many of the American servicemen attended the local hop every Saturday night, and of course plenty of fights took place between them and our British soldiers, for there was much jealousy over girls, and they must have thought they were worth fighting over. Two of the girls I knew married American servicemen, and one a Canadian. Four of my sisters married servicemen who did their part for our country, and thank God they all came home safely to them.

Mr. Bentinck, this is my story – one of a naive country girl, pitchforked into the real world at the age of twenty. I shall never forget those days of fear, but if you feel my story is too tame then just burn it. I know that you wanted stories from ordinary ladies, and that's what I am, and will always be proud of the part I played in our country's dig for victory.

Yours Sincerely,

Mrs. N. Farrow.

P.S. Please do forgive my shaky handwriting, but I have just come out of hospital, after having an operation. My husband, who is a diabetic, has had a leg amputated and is almost blind, but we are still so very happy together, although we now live in a warden-controlled old peoples bungalow. And, yes, we love it!

Letter from Edna Wilde, Hallow, Worcester.....

Dear Mr. Bentinck,

Ref a letter I read in our Evening News, and your programme on BBC Hereford and Worcester, about wartime women. I don't know if this is the kind of information you seek, but here goes.....

I lived in Hull, Yorkshire and worked for the Elastoplast people at the Hessle Road branch, and though wound dressings were badly needed, it was not classed as war work, so at the age of 21 I was called up to play my part for King and country. Many of my friends had been transferred to Coventry to work on aircraft, and I was hoping to join them, but at my interview a girl of my own age snootily told me that as I wasn't very good at anything I would have to go shell filling at Leeds. My heart dropped for I had seen these girls who came home at weekends, with powder burns on their hands and eyelashes, their front hair burned off, and their skin a bright yellow. After an argument about wanting to go into aircraft work, Miss Snooty told me she would send me to Leeds for eight weeks training, and if I passed all the set tests, I would be given a job of some sort in engineering. I learned to file straight, read a micrometer, use pvc bars, sharpen milling dies on a grinder, etc. My maths were good and I could also read technical drawings so I found myself placed in the tool room of Blackburn Aircraft at Brough near Hull, working a flat bed grinding machine. My clocking on time was 7.30am meaning I had to catch the 6.10am bus into Hull, then the train for Brough, followed by a ten minute walk to the factory. We worked a twelve hour day from Monday to Friday, and Saturday and Sunday we worked from 7.30am until 4pm. There were six of us girls in the tool room – two on bench work, two on sharpeners, and two on grinding work. We were treated like fourteen-year-old apprentices, and I admit we did look more like boys in our dungerees, and caps that hid all our hair. We were also told many times that men didn't want us girls in their workshops. Things slowly settled down though, and we were treated very well, and I enjoyed the work of tooling and jigging, which was for the Fleet Air Arm, for the 'Buchaneer' fighter plane.

I joined the St John Ambulance brigade and passed my tests for first aid and home nursing, plus blood donor duties. We would stay one whole night a week on air raid duty and, after the war, Hull City councillors sent a gilded certificate to thank everyone who had helped in any way towards the war effort.

I hope this has been of some interest to you, for it was four years and four months of my life.

I wish you every success with your books, and remain.

Yours sincerely,

Edna M. Wilde.

Letter from Mrs. R.M.E. Webb, Kent.....

Dear Sir,

I have heard you now a few times on BBC Radio Kent, and always find the programmes you take part in of great interest. I thought I would send you just a little tale which might amuse you.

During the war I was in the ATS. I did three weeks basic training at Pontefract, Yorkshire, after which we all had to assemble in the main hall for our posting. There were around 100 of us in all. The posting officer called out Coxon, Middleditch, Derbyshire. I then heard a voice say, "Middleditch? I've never heard of the bleeding place". I looked around and saw a big buxom wench standing behind me – and there was I, a little scrap of nothing. I was terrified, so quickly stepped in front of my kit bag, which read in huge black letters 'Pte. R.M.E. Middleditch, W119266'. Then I heard an officer say, "ah, Coxon. Where are you off to then?' to which she replied, "Middleditch, ma'am, though I've never heard of the place ma'am", so the officer said "come along with me and we will have a look at the map", which was a huge great wall map. I made my way off to the desk to draw my railway warrant and money, which was all of sixpence allowance. I then found that the paperwork had been misread, and we were, in fact, to be posted to Buxton. So I plucked up courage and approached the couple who were scanning the large wall map looking very puzzled, and said, "Excuse me. Are you private Coxon?" She replied "yes, I am". I said "I am private Middleditch and we two are off to Buxton, Derbyshire". I will never forget the look on her face – she was so astonished. But we set off on our journey and you could not have wished for a better, or nicer, person. We became the best of friends, and enjoyed our time in the forces together.

I've told this little tale many times now in my life, and each person has been tickled pink by it. In time I was happy to get married and change that awful name of Middleditch which had caused me so much embarrassment over the years.

Do well with your book, and I hope it will be well advertised, as I for one would love to read it. Also I thank you for all you do to put us ladies on the map for, as you say, we have marked the paths of history, and have done our best to serve our country.

With kind regards,
Mrs. R.M.E. Webb.

Letter from Mrs. June Irons, Swaffham Bulbeck, Cambridge.....

Dear Mr. Bentinck,

Thank you so much for your nice letter. I was most surprised to hear from you, for I have often heard you on Richard Spendlove's programme, and Mandy Morton's programme on BBC Radio Cambridgeshire, and I must say I find your talks so very interesting too. I have often heard you read letters out that you have received from girls who would have been in the Land Army at the same time that I was. As you will know, there were many girls from this area who joined the Women's Land Army. I still keep in touch with some of them, and visit one who lives in Swaffham Prior every month, when we chat over old memories, and always have a good laugh over some of the things we had to do.

I was called up for the war effort in 1942 and decided to join the Land Army; if not that, then I would have liked to join the Wrens, but I had the medical for the Land Army and passed it so in I went. I was sent to Norfolk to work with the timber corps, I only stayed a week though as my billet was a very old nissen hut, and my bed was so damp, that I packed my bags for home. The war agriculture, as it was called then, allowed me to stay at home for a week before they posted me to Swaffham Prior to a hostel for the Land Army, which was the home of Squire Allix, and which today is the home of the Marshall family. There were 60 of us girls in the hostel, all from Liverpool and Manchester – we had a good time together I can tell you. When I left home my mother had said to me, "you won't stick it for long – you don't like to get your hands dirty!" but I showed them and stuck it out for 4 years of my life. I would do it all again tomorrow, if I was younger. We were taken to work in a lorry which was driven by concientious objectors, and we were divided into two gangs and sent to the fens to riddle potatoes, hoe and single out sugar beet, dig carrots out of the ground etc, but this was always in the winter time, and oh how cold it can be in the fens. Sometimes the ground was so frozen that we had to use pick axes to get the produce out. Our hands and fingers also suffered very badly owing to the frost. I remember one Saturday morning we were down on Burwell Fen, and one of the girls, who had not been married for long, lost her wedding ring. All of us spent hours searching for it all to no avail because, as you know, fen soil is so fine and soon covers over (I often wonder if anyone has ever found it in these modern days of metal detectors, for I would have thought it would have come to the surface by now). I remember going back to the hostel at night when we all looked like we had been up a chimney, for the dark soil got everywhere, so you can imagine us sixty girls all wanting a hot bath. Of course, if we were lucky enough to get one, we were only allowed the wartime ration of 5" of water, so you couldn't lay back and relax in it – there was just enough to wash in.

In the summer we did the harvesting and I remember when one poor girl stuck a fork right through her foot (accidently of course). There really was panic stations as we all tried to help her. You can imagine how it was once some of the girls saw the sight of blood – they just fainted, as some did just seeing the fork through her foot.

We also planted trees down in the fens to help as windbreaks. When I have been down in the fens in later years I have been amazed that these trees are still standing, and now of course they are so very big. You must remember that when we planted them all those years ago, it was a bit hit-and-miss for us girls really. We also had to dig out "bog oaks" from the ground – that's trees that have stood the floods of years gone by, and over the years have risen more to the top soil, I can remember when we had dug right down around the stumps, we used to shout to one another that the hole was so deep nobody could see us (very eerie). We would pick potatoes, and put them in large baskets, which when full we would leave to be collected by trailer and tractor. The tractor would spin the potatoes out of the ground and we would walk behind, filling the baskets with them.

We worked with German prisoners of war while at Burwell Fen, and the prisoners would get us the empty baskets and help us with heavy lifting, but the Italian prisoners would just throw one right at you – they weren't as polite as the German prisoners were. We were working a field one day and one of the girls waved to planes that flew over head, for we could see the pilots, quite plainly, in their cockpits. One of them flew over again very low (showing off I suppose) but thank God it was one of ours for the girl kept waving, and he came over so low that he caught her arm with the tip of his wing. Thankfully she was not hurt and it was more of a fright then anything else for her, but I bet it's been a wartime story she has told from that day on. As for me I have been with friends a few times to the Albert Hall in London for a few reunions, and when we sang "God save the Queen" it always brought a lump to my throat, to hear all those fellow former Land Army girls singing together – it really was a bit nostalgic. I like to think that we all did our best to help our country win that vital victory, and I was proud to be a Land Army Girl.

Please do let me know once your book is ready, and please excuse my spelling mistakes, I blame my age now.

I send you my kindest regards,

June Irons.

P. S. On one occasion we were sent to a racing stables at Newmarket, to pick up and remove stones from the paddocks, so that the horses wouldn't hurt their feet. To this day I don't really know what it had to do with the war effort, but it did make a change for us.

Letter from Mrs. M. Danby, Rochford, Essex.....

Dear Mr. Bentinck,

I have read your article in the evening echo, and heard your programmes on BBC Radio Essex, with Steve Screwton, about the subject of World War II. I wondered if you would be interested in hearing about my wartime job.

I had two young sons, aged 7 and 5 years old in 1939, who were evacuated to Derbyshire, and as my husband was on active service, I decided to volunteer for the war effort. I ended up being sent to Cambridge to work for Pye, and even did heavy work at times making spare parts for tanks etc. This proved to much for me, so I was transferred to the assembly line for radio work etc, which I liked. One day our charge hand brought us a huge basket of metal objects which I had to work on. They were about 9 to 10 inches long and 3 inches square with a little opening which looked like a little square window. I had to fix tiny screws and bolts inside these objects, with a very tiny box spanner – it really was so very difficult as the screws and nuts were so small. It was a painstaking job, but at least a clean one. I asked my charge hand what they were for and she replied with one word – 'secret'. We were all curious as we had to work behind a 9ft screen, and were told not to talk to anyone about what we were working on. Then one day we had a V.l.P. visit us who told us to turn out as many as we could. We later learnt that our V.l.P. was none other than the Duke of Kent, who was to die in an air crash just two days later on a trip up north. Later we heard that our secret work was connected with radar, which was to be fitted into the fighter planes. I would like to think that I helped the airman's lot at this time, and I often wonder how many of those brave lads I might have helped stay alive.

I am now 86 years old and housebound owing to spinal damage. I know my story may not be very interesting, and perhaps it doesn't sound very exciting, but I can still recall seeing those poor lads shot out of the skies, as I am sure that you have in films. So many of them were badly burnt up, but once they recovered many of them came to Pyes to watch us work, and they told us just how much our work meant to them. I have since read the war books which have said how radar changed the face of air fights, and I would like to think this is true, because I and the other eleven girls in my team at Pye, worked very hard indeed to do our bit for the war effort.

I wish you the best of luck with your new book, and really look forward to reading it if I am still alive, and kicking.

Yours sincerely,

Minnie Danby.

Letter from Mrs. J. Jones, Keyworth, Nottingham.....

Dear Mr. Bentinck,

Sadly I never heard your programme on our BBC Radio Nottingham with Jeff Owen, when you spoke of your next book on wartime women, but a friend of mine told me how good it was, and gave me the gist of it. So I rang BBC Nottingham, and they were kind enough to give me your address, and told me you would be pleased to hear from me.

I am pleased to enclose the story of my time as a Land Army girl, and hope it will be of help to you, and I look forward to the release of your new book about what we ladies did for the war effort.

Yours sincerely,

Mrs. Joan Jones.

The following is the story by Mrs. Jones, and her thoughts on the progress of farming over the last 50 years.

THE WOMEN'S LAND ARMY

The Cause: We had discussed it – our local boys had volunteered and gone away – we were determined to do our bit; (plus the fact we were eighteen years old, itching to rid ourselves of strong parental control and strike out for ourselves). Being three strong, healthy, enthusiastic young city girls, we were ready for adventure! We set off for the Navy Recruitment Centre full of fire: the centre was closed! Catastrophe! No! The W.L.A. Office was almost next door and, sooner than be daunted, that was our second choice. The interviewer was very keen and helpful and we emerged from the centre, (two of us) signed up members, very elated and ready to go.

Our friends gave us a lovely farewell party and then, having discarded our 'civvies', we were collected by our prospective employer.

The Farm: Our destination, a remote farm, two and a half miles from the nearest village which, we were later to learn, was about the last place God made and even He didn't stay to finish it. Miles and miles, or as we were to learn, acres and acres, of lush, green fields and shady, leafy trees, but oh, so far from the city! (Actually, only twelve and a half miles, we discovered). We shared a comfortable, old-fashioned bedroom in a small cottage and were to be catered for by the farm foreman's wife.

We were up at 6.30am the next morning, dressed in breeches, thick socks, heavy boots, light shirts, beautiful green thick jumpers, overalls, smocks and felt hats! When we viewed each other we fell about laughing – stylish!

Having breakfasted, we set out for the meeting with the boss. He stood in the stackyard with a watch in his hand. "Good morning." "Good morning!" we answered dubiously. His next comment was to inform us that we would start promptly at 7 o'clock each morning, any minutes late would be added up and taken from our weekly wage which was the staggering sum of £1 8s 0d per week, less insurance, and 18s 0d board and lodgings. Then he began his orders for the day.

"I want you to go to the 'fodderum' (fodder-room), get a hayfork, go under the Dutch barn and get a bale of barley straw and take it into the crew yard and spread it out for the beast!!!"

Our mouths dropped wide open – we thought he was foreign (or we were). Years later when recalling this initiation we could laugh but at that moment we were flabbergasted. A grinning toothless labourer came and showed us the procedure but we quaked when we eventually faced the beasts in the yard – we'd never come face to face with these ferocious creatures before and we were for giving the whole project up immediately.

Having survived the first hour, our next experience was the potato pie – not the sort one eats – the one that is in the field. Tons and tons of potatoes covered over with straw and earth which is opened up each day and the contents sorted and bagged ready for the market lorries coming to be loaded. Our main occupation for the next month

108

was potato riddling and bagging. We then progressed to hoeing; acres and acres of young wheat, barley and oats. It was never-ending! Our backs, arms, feet and hearts ached, but we sang and laughed, much to the amazement of the hardened labourers, whom we thought secretly admired us for being so cheerful. Weeks passed by, each day getting a little warmer and easier; we made hay, we harvested, then back to the potatoes – picking this time.

As autumn came we were to experience many various routine procedures of the farming life: stone picking – mainly on wet days when there was nothing under cover to do and if you took it into your head to call it a day the farmer didn't have to pay you! Kale cutting – when the thick, heavy leaves held the water of the previous downpours and we went back to the cottage soaked to the skin. Digging out dock weeds round the edges of the fields – their roots seemed to be fathoms deep. Hedge slashing and dykeing – most inspiring when you are up to your knees in snow or mud!

Needless to say, we did have some relaxation, if it was only to borrow a couple of cycles and pedal to the village – a straggling little place with four pubs mainly used by airmen from the nearby airfield, soldiers from a neighbouring camp and local farm workers. (At that time we were the only W.L.A.). We would have a couple of drinks and then call to see if the local fish and chip shop was open, then cycle back to the farm, much to the disgust of our hostess. Her evening's entertainment consisted of listening to Flanagan and Allen's recording of 'Run Rabbit Run' on the radiogram until 9 o'clock, when she served bread and cheese and hot cocoa, listened to the day's radio news and then went to bed. For city girls this was not amusing!

The farm was largely arable but our boss did buy lambs from Scotland each year. He would graze them to fatten and sell. One evening we had just finished tea when he came to the cottage and asked us to go with him to the village. We rode in the car to the local railway station and on the sidings was a whole train load of lambs waiting to be driven to the farm. Trying to drive sheep that had been shut up a long time, with no food or water, proved to be arduous to say the least. It was pouring with rain that evening. There was the foreman, a dog and two inexperienced land girls (the farmer had departed in his car!). Two and a half miles of main road with deep, wet grass verges proved too tempting to those poor hungry lambs; we whistled, we yelled – darting about like maniacs every time we came to an opening – and finally succeeded the round-up at about 10.30pm, drenched to the skin.

As we were about to leave for the fields one morning, the farmer called to me saying he had a special little job in the yard for me. I was relieved to be rid of the monotonous routine of field work and went willingly. In the stackyard were some old wooden sheds used for storing. He opened the door of one and there, on the floor, lay a sheep. At first I thought it was ill, but he quickly dispelled that thought by telling me he wanted me to pull the wool off its body and put it in a bag, then load the carcass on a barrow, take a spade, dig a hole and bury it! I was nearly as mortified as the poor sheep. I couldn't move. He assured me it wouldn't hurt me – it was dead – and with that comment he walked away! Apart from flies on sticky-paper I'd never seen a dead object before. I was absolutely petrified and gingerly walked nearer to it. The stench was terrible, but I resolved not to be laughed at by the labourers, but to prove I could do it. I timidly pulled away at the wool, and suddenly, the wretched thing seemed to move and emit an enormous belch! I moved fast – so fast I nearly didn't negotiate the door. I shook from head to foot, expecting it to run after me I think. After hanging about for a few minutes, I gingerly crept back – it was still lying there – so once more I pulled wool. Eventually, having buried it, I went to join the others in the field – the men smirked – my friend nearly burst her sides. (A few weeks later there was another plucking session, but it was my turn to laugh because the boss selected my friend to do the chore – 44 years on and she still hasn't eaten lamb!!!).

Needless to say, after both episodes the farm dog scratched up the carcasses and we both had to help re-inter them.

After an experience like that, one needed a bath but, to get that commodity, water needed to be pumped, a copper filling and a fire making under it. A bath taken in the old wash-house, with a rickety wooden door and clear glass window which had to be covered by old sacks, was far from luxury, but very necessary.

Hostel Life: We had heard that there was to be a W.L.A. Hostel built in the village, to be run by the Y.W.C.A. and the County War Agricultural Committee. It was to accommodate fifty girls for group seasonal employment on farms. There were to be dormatories, baths, showers, facilities for washing and drying clothes and a reacreation room. This sounded good, so we immediately applied to the W.L.A. Headquaters to be transferred – the farmer was not too happy about it but, when we got permission to move in, *we* were! Life was different already. We went out in groups – girls of an age – city souls together.

We had some very gruelling, dirty jobs: like – threshing; sileage making; even road making when snow and ice prevented working on the land. Two of us ran an entire pig farm for weeks when the farmer, a single man, was seriously ill. We helped vets with artificial insemination and T.B. testing of cows. We helped deliver lambs; hand-milked cows; fed chickens, horses and beast.

Stooking corn was an art – making four pairs of sheaves stand in a neat little stook – fingers sore with grasping the binder string, and not finishing until every sheaf was off the ground at night. Days seemed endless at harvest time.

Nights in the Hostel could be amusing when quite a lot of girls got together – singing round a piano, or dancing to records (bought by collecting two-pence a week from each member) played on an old wind-up gramaphone. Some nights we organised Whist Drives and invited villagers to play – those nights proved very successful and we raised quite a lot of money for different charitities or the War Effort.

Many girls met their future husbands in the village – army, airforce, farmers – and many still live locally.

As the seasons and the years passed, country life became very acceptable – one was able to perform most jobs proficiently. Sitting in an open field one day, milking one of a herd of cows that grazed some way from the farm buildings, an aircraft pilot came hedge-hopping his plane over the landscape. The sudden roar of the engines didn't meet with the approval of the cow. Up went her heels, the bucket, the milk and me!!! He could have chosen a different route! Farm workers and air pilots had one thing in common – both enjoyed wide open spaces.

1944 was a year of expectancy for us on the land – there was considerable air activity and a good harvest; rumours were passed that the war could soon be over. When the fateful day eventually arrived, May 1945, the girls from the Hostel had been invited to a dance at a local army camp. There had been tension for days, and when the C.O. came into the dance to announce the news everyone went wild with excitement. At the Hostel next morning there were celebrations and everyone rushing to pack their bags ready to depart for home – the city. Of course, after the jubilations work still had to be done, but although most girls didn't leave till after the final victory, V.J. Day, life didn't seem the same. We harvested, thatched, threshed, picked the potatoes and dug more ditches – so the work went on.

My own departure from the land came in 1947 – very sadly in some ways.

Life in the city, for me at any rate, was never the same again.

J. Jones (née Bottemore)

PROGRESS

I stood by the gate and watched the machine. I was quite fascinated by the performance, and it set me thinking how far we had travelled in fifty years. The seasons were the same; the fields were the same; the crops, the dust, the noise; but the performance...

My mind travelled back to the same scene 50 years earlier. I well remember being one of a party of about ten people working in the harvest field. Everyone in shirt sleeves, picking up the sheaves as a windmill-like machine threw them out. Generally a hardworking, intimate, jovial atmosphere, but a determined bunch of individuals trying to get all the sheaves into stooks before rain and darkness descended. Then, after a spell of time, attacking the field again, this time with pitchforks to pick up and load the sheaves onto horse or tractor drawn drays to be carried to the stockyard.

Making a stack and thatching it against the winter weather was a true art such as is seldom witnessed today. The beauty of a newly thatched stack was lovely to see and most farms had several of these in and around their yards. Then, probably months later, all was hustle and bustle again when the great threshing machine was pulled into the stackyard and either steam engine or tractor was hitched to it to drive the huge belts of the machine which threw out the grain into sacks suspended on one end of the machine, and the straw to be stacked again at the other end. Once more involving ten people; a dusty, dirty procedure, but as before, shared by a jovial intimate group of performers.

Now, my mind re-alerted by the innovative machine coming back past the field gate, I was back to my marvelling today. One man, one machine, hours instead of months, and the whole operation was concluded. But how lonely the driver of the machine must feel, alone in the cab, headphones to shut out the constant noise, and eyes glued to the field to prevent straying out of line; depositing the grain into a waiting loader every time round the field and throwing the straw into loose lines to be set on fire when the operation was completed.

Progress, certainly. Picturesque, certainly not.

Joan Jones.

Letter from Doreen Beale, Romney Marsh, Kent.....

Dear Michael Bentinck,

I listened with great interest when you appeared on our BBC Radio Kent the other day. When you said you would like to hear from ladies who did their bit for King and country in World War II, I thought "what about 'The Civil Nursing Reserve' which I joined in November 1942.

We did two weeks training at a London hospital, the one I went to was the Central Middlesex. I stayed in the Civil Nursing Reserve until it disbanded. Recently there was a question in the 'Best of British' magazine, asking if it was countrywide, or only in the Midlands, so I answered it and have since had contact from others who served in nursing. When it really started I do not know, but we did have a uniform – our top coat and hat were air force blue with a red braid on them. We would help out in hospitals, and were always on call to help when a troop train was expected, but many times when I was sent to meet one of these, it was often diverted because of bombing raids, and when they did get through you can imagine the scenes – on a cold station platform, at times many needed urgent medical attention, and it was a pleasure to do your best to help some brave young soldier who had given so much for his country. It really was a very hard life, the nursing was very intensive and we only had a half day off a week. Today they don't know what nursing is with all the modern gadgets to help one – if only we had been able to have some of it in those wartime days, it would have helped us to save so many more lives. When the Civil Nursing Reserve disbanded I became an Enrolled Assistant Nurse and continued to work in nursing until 1961. In your book of ladies' true

stories, I hope you will be able to mention us nurses, and the part we gave for King and country.
I wish you all the very best with it, and am,
Yours sincerely,
Doreen Beale.

Authors Reply:
Dear Doreen, As you will see from the above I have included your letter to me, which I was pleased to receive and also pleased to include. I feel sure that readers of this book will know only too well the wonderful job that you nursing angels did in World War II, and still do to this day. I myself will never forget the day I sat beside my dear late father's hospital bed, when he shared that horrific story with me of how he had seen the poor young nurses of Alexandra Hospital raped and mutilated by Japanese soldiers, just before the fall of Singapore in 1942. He had told me only days before that these young nurses had helped save his life. I know it was something he could never forgive the Japanese for, and although he saw many horrific things in the seven months that he had to drive and assist the Japanese executioner for Singapore, it was this scene that caused him so many nightmares until the day he died. As he was telling me this very moving story, we were both in tears, and yes, it was the nurses around us at the time who comforted us, but at the time my father and I dare not tell them why we were crying. A few years later I received a letter from these nurses, for they had read my book 'My Dad My Hero" and had read the part I mention above, and of course they were horrfied to read what had happened to those brave young nurses. They told me they knew then why my dad and I were crying that day in hospital. Since that time I have spoken to men who have shared some wonderful stories with me of how they owe their lives to a nurse, or, as they put it, 'their saving angel'. Through the paths of history since man began fighting wars, there of course has always been a place for you wonderful nurses, and knowing man's inability to live in peace with one another, I dare say that as time goes by many other young angels will be so needed to suffer for their chosen career. I thank you Doreen, for the part you and all your fellow nurses played in giving us our today.
Yours most sincerely, Michael Bentinck.

Letter from Mrs. Barbara J. Winter, Royston, Herts.....

Dear Mr. Bentinck,

I really did enjoy listening to you on Radio Cambridge talking about Land Army girls. I always like to hear you with Mandy Morton, for you are both so good on the subject of wartime stories. You may remember I spoke to you after the programme on the telephone, then afterwards I spoke to my mum, Mrs. Gladys Graham (née Schofield) who came from Bermondsey, south London. She went to the labour exchange to enquire about what she could do to help the war effort and asked about any thing concerning the Land Army. She was then signed up and sent to March near Ely to work on a fruit farm where she spent all her time picking fruit, and caring for the fruit trees etc. It was very hard work for her with long hours, and very early starts each day. After coming from London, I imagine it must have been very strange for her being in the country, after the busy sights of our capital city.

Her two best friends, Lilly and Rosey, went to work in a village called Waterbeach, near to Cambridge, where they both met and married Americans, who were stationed nearby. Mum stayed in a hostel, which she thinks was at the back of March High Street. She married my dad in 1943 – in her Land Army uniform. She has often made me laugh with the following tale, for she had never ridden a bike in her life until she went into the Land Army, and was issued with a bike to get from the hostel to the farms where she was required to work. She had to ride down a steep hill to get to work, and at the bottom of the hill was a fish shop, which had a big glass front window. Mum tells me she still wonders to this day how she never went head first through this window, for she could never stop the bike once it built up speed, however hard she pulled up on the brakes, and if wet of course it made it even worse for her. She would often fall off of her bike and break her flask – she lost count of how many of them she broke, which she had to pay for, but the worst thing was having to go with out a drink all day. Thankfully she never did hit the fish shop window, but came close to it on many occasions, when the fish shop owner would be as relieved as mum was that she had lived to ride another day in one piece. I can just see this young red head " whizzing" down that hill. If nothing else, those war years must have taught mum to ride a bike, for it was only a few years ago that she hung up her cycle clips, and put her bike riding days behind her. After my dad came out of the army I was about one year old, (I was born 1947) and dad wanted to get out of London, so we moved to Arrington, where dad got a job on the land. There was an American camp here, and I bet the wartime locals could tell you some stories about what went on. My mum and dad went on to settle in Melbourn, where they still live today. I really would appreciate it if you could mention my dear mother in your new book, and I thank you for all you do for that wonderful generation of people that gave and suffered so much for us younger ones to have a good life today.

Yours sincerely,

Mrs. Barbara J. Winter.

Letter from Mrs. Topsy Price, Ross On Wye, Herefordshire.

Dear Michael Bentinck,

I found your article in the local press, and your programme on BBC Hereford and Worcester, of great interest for I too was a Land Army girl. As you said, you have had many Land Army stories told to you, but I hope the two I relate to you here will be a little different.

The first was in the summer of 1940 at Chepstow, a man with Fox Photo credentials came to the farm where I was working, and asked permission from my boss and myself to take some photos for publicity purposes, to help the war effort. He returned later and gave me four excellent large photos, and then took even more (I enclose one for you to see). I never had these for long because soon afterwards the police arrived and questioned me at great length. It turned out that the photographer was a spy. There was a munitions factory near to us and he had been caught in the factory taking photos. Of course, when the police processed the film they found photos of me, and so thought I was a suspect. Oh, how bad I felt, for I was just a young girl doing her bit for King and country, and this man had played on my naivety, but I can assure you I became very wary of suspicious looking people after that. The second event was in 1943 when I was asked to represent our county at a garden party at Buckingham Palace. To be presented to the Queen was just so wonderful, but the added bonus was to meet the little princesses. I still have the invitation card, and the press cuttings relating to that wonderful day, and of course many memories of all that happened. Like all my fellow Land Army comrades we played our part to keep our country going, when the odds were stacked against it, and our men folk were fighting to keep us free.

I thank you for your kindness, and interest in the part us girls played in World War II, and I hope these stories will be of help to you.

Yours sincerely,

Topsy Price.

Letter from Mrs. Hazel Harris, Worcester.....

Dear Sir,

Having read your article in the Worcester Evening News, with reference to Land Army girls in World War II, I thought you might be interested in the enclosed poem. It was written for my friend Marg and I, when we served in the Women's Land Army on a big farm in North Herefordshire from 1939 until 1941. Here we tended Hereford cattle, sheep, and worked with grain, potatoes and sugar beet, which were all produced abundantly to help feed the British folk. The work was mainly carried out by eight pensioners and us two girls, as the younger men had all previously joined up to fight for our country. Then one day our local road man came to work with us for a few months before his call up came through. Cliff was his name – a married man with a young family, so consequently he looked out for Marg and I, and looked after us, and helped us with heavy lifting, and saw we came to no harm. Anyhow, when he left to go off to fight for our country, he asked us if we would write to him and keep him informed of the village news, which of course we did. Cliff was drafted abroad, I don't know where to, as his address was British Forces Post Office, (B.F.P.O.). Then one day around the middle of 1941, the enclosed poem arrived, which he had dedicated to us.

The war finally ended and Marg and I got on with our lives. We both got married and raised our families. As for Cliff, he too had moved on, and I never heard of or saw him again. Then one day in 1991, out of the blue, I was visited by his son who, of course, I didn't even know. He informed me that Cliff had died in 1989, and as he had always spoken to his family about his days on the farm with Marg and I, his son thought that he would find us and let us know of Cliff's death, which was so very good of him.

Now back to my Land Army days.... Gosh, didn't we have to work hard – our boss expected us to do twice as much work as the old pensioners did, with no extra pay I might add, but we were fortunate to be able to stay at home to live with our families, which made up for everything. We were able to cycle to work, which meant a very early start as most mornings we had to be at the farm by 6.00am. Marg did a lot of work with this darn great carthorse, and I did the tractor work and ploughing etc. One day at sheep-shearing time, the boss told Marg and I to help the men with the sheep. The ewes had already been shorn, so we had to tackle the lambs. Our first attempts took the men by surprise to say the least, for we were using a bright orange dye to mark the sheep with, and we got it all over the men as well, much to the amusement of everyone going past on the nearby road. It took months for this colour to wear off, and so caused quite a few laughs in the village to see all these orange coloured men walking about the place. What a shame we have no photos of it, but I don't think many people had a camera in those days let alone a film to put in it.

Marg and I still meet up quite often and laugh about our Land Army days, and we recall the days we got soaked to the skin through working in the rain all day long, or from being soaked in sweat while haymaking, and corn harvesting, and those awful weeks (or months) of threshing. Of course there were no labour-saving implements in those days, with most jobs being done by hand (I wonder if the young ones of today would do it all). There are many other incidents we recall when we are together. I must add that this year Marg and her husband celebrate their Golden Wedding, and have been lucky enough to be invited to celebrate with the Queen and Prince Philip at Buckingham Palace.

I've copied out the poem as it was written, as the paper is so thin now and weather beaten. If it's any use to you please do use it.

Yours,
Hazel Harris.

Cliffs Poem to Hazel and Marg, dedicated to the W.L.A.

There's a fine lot of troops in old England today,
And every one thinks that they're grand.
But if anyone wonders "whose best?" I would say
'Tis the lassies who work on the land.
On the farms they work hard in all kinds of weather,
In sunshine or snow they're as good.
They've got "guts", yes they're sure tough as leather
Are those lassies who get us our food.
We've soldiers and sailors and airmen as well,
In that land which I'm proud to call home,
But the Women's Land Army will lick 'em to hell
Though they'd be the last ones to say.
They're on at their tasks and they'll pull us right through
This war, if we keep up our heads.
But were it not for the great work which they so proudly do,
We would lose cause we'd run short of bread.

Letter from Mrs. Connie Peachey, Wisbech, Cambs.....

Dear Michael,
    I know that you will remember me. I have written to you a few
times now, for like your father, my dear late husband was a Far Eastern
Prisoner of War. The other day on BBC Radio Norfolk, I heard you
speaking on your subject of World War II, as usual so very good to
listen to. I thought you might be interested to hear of what I did during
the war. I have enclosed not a very good copy of a group photograph
of C. Company letter section R.E.P.S. Did you know that the army
post office is a part of the Royal Engineers, and that we A.T.S. were
entitled to wear their collar dog bomb on our jackets (though we wore
the A.T.S. cap badge and buttons)? To give you an idea of our numbers,
there were 4 companies in the letters section, at least 2 parcels
companies, an HQ company as well as cooks and mess and billet
orderlies, and added to us there was a pay corps office in Nottingham
itself. Also, quite a few A.T.S. at the big Ordnance Depot at Chilwell

119

and other service installations in the neighbourhood. So you can tell that Nottingham was not short of service personnel.

All the charitable organisations had canteens – very good ones, and any time our cookhouse fare was not up to much, there was no need to go hungry or to pay the earth at the many cafés. Not all the cafés were expensive, and if we were on late shift and fancied a lie in, we would miss breakfast and go down to a café in a small street near to the Empire Theatre, for a cup of tea and two generous slices of lovely buttered toast and marmalade for a tanner (6d).

I have just returned from a week's visit to a friend of mine who, by the way, celebrates her golden wedding anniversary this year. We had some laughs about the strange things that happened and the happy and sad times we all shared together with our mates of that time. We remembered we had one friend in the registered letter enclosure, who was married to a naval officer. When he finally came home on leave, she of course came back to work pregnant and we all watched over her like hawks, until her discharge came through, for we wanted to make sure that she did not lift any heavy mail bags. At this time quite a few girls were engaged to service personnel who were serving in the Middle East, and when that part of the war finished and their men came home, they got married. However, they were soon called to join the nucleus of the "second front" troops, and there was great concern when one of these newly-married girls was widowed, so very soon after the D-Day landings.

We lived mostly in large requisitioned houses, with bare floor boards and with 5 to 8 of us in one room. Another room was kept as a recreation room, where we were allowed to have a fire, which was used for all sorts of tasks, none more than boiling water, for the main boilers were so unreliable – our open fire was just wonderful. If the main boiler couldn't provide us with water to bath in, we were allowed to have a free bath at the nearest public baths. Other than that, if we used the public baths we had to pay 6d, (of course we only got the regulation 5 inches of water) which included a very small piece of soap, and the use of a very rough towel. However, we knew that we were living in luxury compared to the girls on Ack-Ack and searchlight sites – very, very dangerous for them indeed.

It must have been about late 1943 or early 1944 that the N.A.A.F.I. decided to start up a club in a large building near to the city centre.

There were lots of facilities, including rooms where visiting service personnel could stay overnight, and the large Y.M.C.A. also had overnight facilities, so we really were well looked after. There were also quite a few civilian families who welcomed us into their homes. You will have heard how at times of war and great stress, people find a true spirit of comradeship, and so many of the families that invited us into their homes had a son or a loved one fighting, or being held prisoner by the enemy in some foreign land. We wartime women were proud to be doing our bit towards keeping our country free for, as I have heard you say Michael, if Nazi Germany and the hateful Japanese at that time had won the war, then none of us would have the life we do today. So I am proud to say that I played my part for our great Country to remain "free".

With my Best Wishes to you and Hilary,
Connie Peachey.

Authors Reply:
Dear Readers, As you will have read from Connie's letter, her dear late husband was a Far Eastern Prisoner of War, and a comrade of my own dear late father. Connie has kept in touch with me since she read my first book "MY DAD MY HERO". She has kept me informed of how her Wisbech FEPOW Association helps those who are suffering from the mental war trauma and all that goes with having been a prisoner of the Japanese in those nightmare days. One thing she has kept me informed of, which I know she won't mind me sharing with you all, is about her own grandson Charles, who is serving in the Royal Navy on board HMS Illustrious. At the time of writing the Illustrious is on her way home from a tour of the Far East, and as Charles knows only too well of the debt we owe his grandfather and his comrades, he wanted to mark his visit to Singapore, and retrace some of his dear grandfather's footsteps. The following is an extract from Charles' letter to his grandmother Connie:

"On the 30th of April, I went off to Krangi War Memorial. Our ship had organised a wreath-laying ceremony, and act of remembrance. I had spoken to our chaplain about grandad, so he agreed to allow me to lay the ship's wreath. He read out a piece about him on the lines of my note enclosed. I laid the original with the wreath, and it is now kept with the graves register. On the back of it are our addresses. It was a wonderful service, very dignified, but a little emotional. I found the Cambridgeshire remembrance wall of names, and had my photograph taken by the side of it. The cemetery is kept in immaculate condition Gran, a thing all the families of those dear fallen men can be proud of. I also visited the POW chapel at "Changi" prison and had a look round the small museum there. The chapel and museum are very peaceful places now, with lots of association badges on the walls – it really was very interesting, but I could not forget the suffering and torture that my grandfather and his comrades must have suffered within these same walls".

The following are the words on the plaque that Charles left with the wreath:

"FOR THE MEMORY OF OUR GRANDAD. For the memory of the 2nd Cambridgeshire regiment and to the servicemen who gave their lives in Singapore, during World War II. May we all remember them. L/CPL. ALBERT EDWARD PEACHEY. 5932582. Our grandad was born 16.6.1912. He joined the territorial army in Wisbech Cambridgeshire, on 12.2.1934, and was called up to the 2nd Cambridgeshire regiment as a private on 29.9.1939. He was promoted to Lance Corporal in July 1941. He sailed from Gourock, Scotland on the Polish M.V. Sobieski on 31.10.1941 to join the 18th Division convoy, to arrive in Singapore via Newfoundland and South Africa on 13.1.1942. He was sent to Batu Pahat with the 15th Indian Infantry Brigade, and he was ordered to withdraw back into Singapore on 23.1.1942. He saw fighting in the Braddell Road area until the ceasefire was ordered and all troops were taken prisoner on 15.2.1942. He was sent to Changi jail before he started work on the Burma railway. He worked from various prison camps – Tamajoa, Kanburi, Chungkai, Taisan, Kachanburi, to name just a few. He finally returned to England late in October 1945, and was transferred after leave to the Reserves on 11.2.1946. Our grandad always wanted one day to revisit Singapore, but sadly he never made the journey, for sadly he passed away quietly at home in Wisbech on 10.9.1982 with his beloved wife Connie, our dear grandmother, beside him to the end. My brother and I miss him so very much.

Charles and Martin Wicks – Grandsons"

"I have come to Kranji today, 30.4.97, to pay my last respects to the soldiers who served with him, on his behalf. I am Charles Wicks LRO, Royal Navy, HMS lllustrious.

Authors comments:
Dear Connie, Thank you so very much for sharing your story of your wartime days. I wonder how many of our dear boys received a letter from their loved ones thanks to the part you and your army post office girls played in getting the mail through. I can also see how proud you are of your grandsons, and I know how proud their granfather would be of them, for as Charles laid that plaque of remembrance, he was saying thankyou, from all of us who owe our lives to those brave men.

Letter from Mrs Norah Beaumont, Worsley, Manchester.....

Dear Mr Bentinck,
    I heard your interview today, 29th October 1997, on BBC Radio Merseyside, with Linda Mc Dermott. It was so very good, and it is always good to hear your programmes based on World War II. I hope you will remember me, for you were kind enough to speak to me when I rang you after the programme – thanks for listening to my tales. I hope you will find the following of interest. It is just a little of my wartime life....
    I am a showman's daughter, and when war broke out I went to work in a factory as my way of helping my country. I stuck it for about two years but with me not being used to working inside and being closed in I just had to pack it in, as it was making me ill. So one day I was walking down the road when I saw a lorry with farm produce on it and I thought "that's it! Someone has to grow and collect our crops. I'll see if I can have a go at that". I set off for the labour exchange and told them I thought I would like to join the W.L.A. (Women's Land Army). After sorting things out I set off for home to tell my mum and dad. My dad said "I'll give you a week, and you'll want to come home". My friends laughed and wondered if I had gone mad. They all said "you won't stick that job one minute". I said to myself "I'll show them

and stick at it even if just to prove them wrong". I was sent to a place called Usk in Wales. I had never heard of the place before – only husk I knew of was the husk on a coconut. Well I found Usk alright and got off the bus outside the Institute. It reminded me of my schooldays, when I was a boarder at a convent. I walked up the driveway and there I saw some boys digging and I asked one of them the way to the matron's office. He asked me how long was I in for? I looked at him dumbstruck and asked him what he meant, and he told me that he was a borstal boy. I stared at him and said "are you being funny?", and walked away. Well, I met the matron and she told me what I had to do and what not to do whilst waiting for tea time. I had a stroll round and I thought to myself "I'll never stick this" as I was used to the bright lights and noise of the fairground. Tea time came and I met the girls – they seemed to me a nice crowd. A week went by and I was feeling homesick, but I said to myself "I'll stick at it and see it through if it kills me". I was put on to tractor work which was strange to me after driving a car. One day they sent me with another girl to do some ploughing – neither of us knew anything about it but they told us the farmer would help us. He was very nice and showed us how to start the work. To think we knew nothing about the land, and what I know today is hard to believe.

At the Institute we used to do a fire watch once a month. One day they asked for volunteers to join the decontamination squad, so eight of us joined. I was the stoker on the boiler for hot water for any possible casualties. One afternoon we had to give a demonstration and I couldn't get the fire going, but I remembered some old oil in the workshop and oh boy, did that water get hot that day! We have had many a laugh about it since then. We had many good times, so it was not all hard work – we went to dances, and film shows, and we did our best to put on shows to entertain the wounded servicemen. Altogether we enjoyed our stay at Usk very much.

Once they told us we were moving to another place but nothing came of it, then one day in July they again said we were moving. We all laughed and said we have heard that one before, but alas this time it was true, and we were so sorry that we had to leave, but we didn't mind so much once we heard that servicemen were taking our places. On Friday July 13th 1945 we all went out to celebrate our stay at Usk. I don't think any of us girls will ever forget our last night there, including Matron, for we said goodbye in style. The Usk,

Monmouthshire Institute of Agriculture provided a happy home for fifty of us Land Army girls, and Michael, we were proud to play our part as War Time Women.
Yours most sincerely,
Norah Beaumont.

P.S. Today, in my eighties, I still proudly march with the Showmans Guild, in London on Remembrance Day, as we pay our respects to those who gave so much for our today. As you say Michael, we can all wear our poppies with pride.

Letter from Mrs Joan Clark, London.....

Dear Michael,
Please do forgive my informality, but I have heard you twice now on radio, here in London – once when you appeared on London News Talk, and once when you were on our Radio Liberty speaking to presenter Simon Bates. I always think how well you speak on the subject of our brave Far Eastern Prisoners of War.
Well, my sister Mavis has told me of the programmes that you do with Mandy Morton, on BBC Radio Cambridgeshire, about War Time Women, and especially on the subject of Land Army Girls, and as she knew I was in the Women's Land Army, and that I had read your books, she said how I should write and share some of my stories with you. That is why I phoned you first to see what you thought about it. As I told you, I am not very good at writing or spelling, and may not be able to make it sound too good, but as you said, that's the part you will help me with. I thought "why not?", so here it is Michael.
The first story I share with you is one that our family has had more laughs over whenever we have been together, at family weddings, or even funerals, than any other wartime story. It is a true story of my dear old grandad. He had fought in the Great War, in the trenches against the hun, and I know you would have liked to hear his many tales of woe. He suffered lung damage, and lost a leg, for the part he played in that campaign. While I was away with the Land Army, my sister Mavis was away as a nurse. I know she has told you how she

nursed those brave boys when they returned at last from the Far East. Our young brother had been evacuated to the country. This left just my mum and dad, and dear old grandad at home, as grandad lived with us since gran had died. One night dad was out doing his air raid wardens patrol, when mother was called to help a neighbour, who was about to give birth. She said to grandad "now you will be all right won't you dad? I've just got to nip round to Ruby's 'cos she's gone into labour, but as it's her fifth, I shouldn't be too long". Ruby only lived a few streets away, and while mum was gone there was a bad air raid – a real bad one – so bad in fact that it took our house right down, with a direct hit. Even the house that mum had gone to suffered bomb damage with all the windows blown out and the main wall cracked wide open. Well once mum got Ruby's baby delivered, which by the way was another girl, she got herself together as best as she could, for I can imagine the shock she must have been in – just imagine delivering a new baby with the house falling down around you. She set off for home and on arrival at the top of our street she could see the carnage that the raid had caused – air raid wardens and our brave firemen were everywhere, plus anyone who could lend a hand – all up to their waists in brick rubble. She was told to get out of the way, as it was no place for a woman, and told to go home, to which she replied "this *was* my home!" They asked her if she knew if anyone else was in the house that night. Mum burst into tears and said "yes, my dear old dad". As she was telling them this, they could hear someone shouting "let me out of this bloody toilet", for all that was left of our house was our old outside toilet, right at the bottom of our garden. Brick rubble and bits of timber had blown up against the door, and yes, imprisoned our dear old grandad inside it.

The firemen clambered away at the rubble and got him out. Grandad, who was deaf, came out shouting "what's all the bloody noise about – all this banging going on. A bloke can't even go to the lavvy in peace!" Once he did calm down and take the time to look around him he couldn't believe just how lucky he was. My mum couldn't speak for crying, and kept cuddling grandad to her. The firemen said "they have bombed your house sir", to which grandad replied, "what them bloody Germans? They just won't leave me alone – they're dead set on getting me, you know. They took me leg off in the last war now the buggers nearly got all of me".

Well after the war, as I have said, whenever our family was all together again it was always this story that we laughed at most, but looking back it could have been a very tragic story, for grandad was lucky.... so many of our dear neighbours were not so fortunate as grandad and died in the carnage that those German bombs caused. As for my grandad he went on to make 89 years of age before he died of old age, but I think it fair to mention that this story got him many a free pint of mild in the new pub that was built on the corner of our street.

While all this was going on, though, I was away working on a farm in Suffolk with two other girls both my age, yes all of twenty. They were Harriet and June – one was from London like me, and the other was all the way from Lancashire. The funniest thing that happened, looking back, was one day when I was feeding the pigs, I had to boil up any old left over food in an old copper, and mix it in with all the pig swill, then I would pour it into their food trough for them to eat. They knew when you had food for them and would rush at you to get it. I was afraid of them really, and used to throw the food into the trough as quickly as I could and then get out. On this day, as I fed them, I rushed out so quickly that I didn't close the gate to the pig sty properly. I went off to join the others out in the fields where, believe it or not, I drove the tractor. We were actually muck spreading – not a very nice job at all, but us girls had to do all farming tasks now. Well after about an hour of doing this the farmer, Mr Groves, came running into the lower field shouting at us, "who's left the bloody gate open to the pig sheds". My two pals looked at me, and I had to say "it must have been me Mr Groves, as I was the one who fed them today". "Well," he said, "you'd better all come with me and help me to get them back again then". We all set off along the road to the village, but soon found that some of them had not gone far. Mr Groves soon rounded them up and got them back into the sty. Four of the large ones were still missing though, so we set off again to search for them. Just up the road from the farm was the vicarage, and here we found them on the vicar's vegetable patch – yes, eating all his wonderful produce. One of the pigs had knocked over the vicar's wife's washing pole, bringing all her washing down, and was dragging all this washing along behind him – it was a sight I shall never forget. I laugh about it now, but at the time I think I cried. The vicar and his wife were so very good about it all and were even laughing at the sight of this pig with a sheet pulled over it, yet still moving along. The following sunday the vicar even used the story in his sermon, when of course Harriet and June told everyone it was my fault not theirs. Anyway, Mr Groves took over the feeding of the pigs from then on, which suited me just fine.

I went on to work on other farms across our country throughout the war, and met some very brave people, and I was proud to do my bit for the war effort. To this day I know how the long hours and hard work that we girls had to do played such a vital part in bringing our great country to victory. As you know, Michael, after the war in 1947, I married my childhood sweetheart Jack, and this year we celebrate our Golden Wedding along with so many other wartime couples. After what my Jack suffered as a prisoner of the Japs, I love him even more, if that's at all possible, for after what he saw and suffered, he has been kindness itself. Such a wonderful man. Yes, I have been kicked out of bed a few times over the years, when he has been gripped by some horrific nightmare because of what he suffered, but we have come through it all together, and we have two wonderful children, and four grandchildren. Yes, I really have been lucky, for I am able to share with you two amusing wartime stories, for my war was so very different from my dear Jack's war. I also thank you for your books, for they have shown my children just how much their father and his comrades went through for them to be here today. God bless you Michael, and keep up the good work.

Yours thankfully,
Joan Clark.

Letter from Molly Benyon, Hull.....

Dear Mr. Bentinck,

I have enjoyed hearing you on our BBC Radio Humberside, with your wonderful talks on World War II. The last time you were on you mentioned that you planned to do a book on the part women played in the war. I rang radio Humberside, and they were kind enough to give me your address, so I thought I would write to you of my main story of that time in my life. The story I have chosen is one that really changed my life, and if you think it will be of help to you please use it in your book.

I was actually working on a farm in Kent at the time along with another Land Army girl called Cissy who has remained a lifelong friend. One day Cissy and I had been hop picking, which was another job we girls had to do, along with those from all walks of life from tramps to gypsies to pensioners, and even prisoners of war. I dare say you will know by now that we really had to be jacks-of-all-trades in our dig for victory. It had been a very hard, long hot day, and to relax once back at the farm where we were staying, Cissy and I would fill a large old galvanized water tank which was in the barn, with water from the farm well. The tank was about 5ft square by about 3ft high, and I can tell you we had more than the 5 inches of water allowed in war time. It was a wonderful hot summer's night – one of those nights when you're too hot and sticky to sleep, so we were happy to just lay and relax in the warm water. While we lay relaxing in the tank, we heard the noise of aeroplane engines droning over head. We just assumed they were our chaps returning after a night-time raid over Germany. Alas, we were wrong, and they turned out to be German bombers on their way to bomb London. Even so, little did we expect what was to follow.... one of them dropped his bombs! We only knew this when we heard the whistling sound that they made as they screamed down to earth. We had no time to run for it and heard an almighty bang, and to be honest I can't remember much more about it than that. I awoke in hospital some time later, and found my legs were in plaster right up to my waist, and the pain I was in I would not wish on anyone.

Some months later I was taken back to the farm to collect my belongings. The barn was just a load of rubble. Cissy and the farmer told me how lucky we had been to get out alive. Cissy had escaped with just bad scratches, and had suffered bad bruising. But the main roof beam had landed on my legs and back, as I had been blown right out of the tank and had landed on the floor, where the beam had come down on top of me. I have of course been left disabled, but I am at least still here and glad to be alive. When people ask me why I am disabled I am always proud to say "oh, these are my war wounds".

I do have more amusing stories to tell you, and will write again soon. Please do keep up your writing, and please do consider my letter for use in your book. I also thank you, Michael, for putting your other books on to tapes for me, for my sight is not too good these days, but thankfully I can still hear a bit – pity I never heard them bombs a bit sooner though!

Best wishes,

Molly Benyon.

Letter from Mrs Elsa Crow, Exeter, Devon.....

Dear Mr. Bentinck,

My friend, Norma, heard you speaking about your books on BBC Radio Devon with Douglas Mounce on his morning programme. She rang me to tell me of your intended book of ladies' wartime stories. As soon as she mentioned your name it rang a bell with me, for only the night before I had read an article that you had written in our local Evening News, about Land Army girls. If my stories are any help to you please do use them in your new book, for I was proud to have been a Land Army girl. I still often have a laugh when I think of the things we got up to – talk about Dad's Army – it's a wonder no one made a TV serial about us girls and the things *we* got up to.

One instance I recall was when I was working on a farm in Devon with two other girls, who were really timber girls who had been working for the forestry commission before coming to work on the farm. They were nice girls and so full of fun, but alas the farmer and his wife were two of the most miserable people God ever put on this earth. They made it clear they didn't like us girls, and that we were only there to work. They were so very tight with their food and I feel sure they begrudged us even what little food they did allow us. One of my duties each morning was to feed the animals and collect the eggs from the hen house. I then had to take them up to the farm house and by the time I got to the house it was mid morning. On this particular morning as I entered I could smell the wonderful aroma of home cooking – it really smelt so very nice. I knew it was a good home made stew cooking on the range. I also knew that it would not be for us girls to eat. As I placed the eggs on the table, I saw a note saying 'George, your dinner is simmering on the range. It is a stew. Help yourself to it, dear, as I shall be eating in town today with my friend Iris. Should be back mid afternoon. Love Jean". I turned to leave the kitchen when a strong impulse came over me.... I thought to myself "why should this tight old so-and-so have all this lovely stew all to himself, when us poor girls never get much more than a bowl of soup?" As I opened the door to leave, the first thing I saw was their pig bin, which was emptied and mixed with the pig's swill. The strong impulse just took me over, and for what I did next may I be forgiven, for I went and got another saucepan and filled it with the pig's swill. I was thinking to myself "that old so-and-so isn't going to have all that stew to himself. It's time me and the girls had something good to eat for a change". I placed the saucepan with the swill in it onto the range and added a drop of the real stew from the other saucepan to try and make it smell a bit better, really. I covered the other saucepan over with a towel, and took it and hid it in the hen house, while I went off to tell the other girls what I had done. They said "good for you, Elsa. My God, we can't wait 'til lunch break now!" As soon as George the farmer went off for his lunch, we girls hurried along to collect our stew. We took it into the barn and indulged ourselves with the best food we had eaten since we left home. It really was so good – it had lovely meat in it, and carrots, onions, swede, parsnips, potatoes, and dumplings.

As we sat and enjoyed our meal, we laughed to ourselves how we hoped old George was enjoying his special stew. We waited until George came out of the farmhouse, and once he was well away from the house, I sneaked back in to wash and replace the saucepan. I looked in the other saucepan which was still on the range, and found that George had eaten most of it, the rest I quickly put into the pig bin, and washed up for him. The next morning George's wife called us to her and said George will be late starting work today as he has not been to good through the night – he'd been in and out of the toilet all night with a tummy upset. "Must be something he's eaten" she said. We girls told her to tell him not to worry as we knew what work needed doing and we would see to it. As we turned to leave the first thing I saw was the pig bin, and oh did I feel bad. The other girls were laughing and they said "Elsa, we don't think we'll be getting another nice lunch today somehow". How right they were, for it was back to soup and bread again for us. Ever since the end of the war, every time I have made a stew for my family, I have had this sense of guilt come over me, as I say, may I be forgiven.

I do remember that on a Saturday night we girls went to the local dance, and on the way we would have a good hot meal at a café in town. It cost us one and a tanner, but was well worth it, for I think it kept us going through those dark days, as they were hard times, with very long hours. I hope we girls played our part though, in feeding the country, even if we did not get fed very well ourselves – it is still the part of my life that I remember most. I thank you for caring about us old ones Michael, and for doing your best to tell the rest of the world about the part us Land Army girls played for our country's victory.

Best wishes,
Elsa Crow.

Letter from Mrs. Margaret Drake, Northampton.....

Dear Mr. Bentinck,

I really do enjoy hearing you on our BBC Radio Northampton, and always find it very moving, but also so very interesting, when you talk about your father's time with the Japanese executioner in World War II. Also, I think it is so important that people know of what he and his comrades went through for us all to have a life today. Also to learn by it, and to never allow such things to happen again. I know that our presenter Anna Murby is only a young lady, but it was good to hear her say how much she had learnt about the war in the Far East, thanks to you being her guest. I have also heard you with Mark Whall on his programme, and as Mark and Anna know, so many brave men from Northamptonshire suffered so much at the hands of the Japanese. It is so hard for them to forget, and certainly to forgive. Your father was indeed a very brave man, and, as you say, so very lucky to be able to move on with his life, and just look for the good in people. I heard you mention to Anna that you were writing a book on the subject of what ladies did in the war, and as I did my bit for the war effort I thought I would drop you a line about it.

I came to Northampton just after the war when I married my husband in 1946, for it was his home town. I myself was born and raised in Nottingham. My father was a greengrocer, and I used to help him on Saturdays and after school, and I learnt much about the veg and fruit trade, so of course the Women's Land Army seemed the right outfit for me to do my bit for King and country. I went to quite a few farms around our great country but the one I remember most was in Wales, not far from Hereford. I remember I stayed in lodgings in a village called Foxley with, I believe, a Mr and Mrs Burrows. I was only here for about six weeks as I was covering for a girl who had been taken ill and had been sent home. I had heard funny stories of the Welsh people and of how they were to us outsiders, but I found them all so kind to me. A Mr Jones used to pick me up with two other girls and take us to the different farms to work. I remember he told us not to keep saying Mr Jones, but to call him Taffy. He was so very kind and even brought enough lunch to share with us girls each day. One day he told us that he had lost his only son early on in the war at the retreat of Dunkirk. He had been shot while waiting on the beaches for his chance to board a ship out. But as you know, the German planes just opened up on our boys as they crowded up the beaches in their efforts to get away. Such easy targets for those German fighter planes, and I know so many of our dear boys died helplessly at that time. He was of course in tears as he told us this, and we said "don't upset yourself, Taffy. Try not to think about it now. You don't have to tell us". He replied "but it helps me to talk and think about my David – he was my life". Well we all sat in this field in floods of tears, for we all felt so much at the heartache he was going through. Many of the village people told us that it had changed Taffy so much, and all he used to talk about was his son and of what they were going to do together after the war. I was not quite 20 years old at this time and I think it fair to say that it was my first insight into realising just how much this war affected innocent people like dear Taffy.

A more amusing story is the one of Mr Burrows, with whom I stayed for this six weeks. His wife had been on to him to sweep the chimneys ready for winter as it was now October and was starting to get very cold in the evenings. Mr Burrows said "they don't need sweeping love. I only did them all last year". Mrs Burrows replied "last year be blowed – it was all of five years ago when you last swept them. I was the one who had to shout to you when the brush came out the top of the chimney". When she said this it brought back happy memories to me how as a child I had to watch outside when my dad swept our chimney, and I would shout and rush into him once I saw the brush stick out the top. Well Mr and Mrs Burrows started to argue over when the chimneys were last swept, and in the end Mr Burrows said "oh alright love, I will do them at the weekend". The following day it was so cold that Mrs Burrows lit a fire in the sitting room, and that evening we all sat round it to keep warm. When it started to die down a bit Mrs Burrows said "the fire's not drawing too good love," to which Mr Burrows replied "must be the direction of the wind tonight love". He said "I know what I'll do – I'll put one of my old worn out boots on it. That'll get it going a bit". Well, he never said a truer word, for he put this old size 10 worn out boot onto the fire, which just blazed up the chimney once it caught alight. The old boot was covered in diesel oil from his old tractor, and I know it had an old paraffin rag in it. Well needless to say in a short while the chimney was alight, and of course we all got out as quickly as we could, amongst the shouting that Mr and Mrs Burrows were doing to one another. Once outside the sparks were streaming out of the chimney. I ran off to fetch help, and within a short time there were many hands to the pump. Mr Burrows had the ladder up to the house and was up on the roof, everyone else was passing buckets of water from the old water pump up to him to pour down the chimney. Well in time the fire was out but once we went inside, the state of the sitting room was like a war zone. Poor Mr Burrows – I don't think he knew what to say to his wife for the best. But she had plenty to say to him, and I bet she did have for some time after. She kept saying to him "who needs the bloody Germans to come bombing us while you're about?" Well, after a couple of weeks I left this happy homestead to return to my own home at Nottingham, and when I told my parents this story they really did laugh.

Once the war finished I left the W.L.A. and went back to help dad with his business, which was where I was to meet my husband-to-be when he walked in the shop and said to me "can I have some of your nice fruit to take home to me mum please". I said to him "where does your mum live then", and he replied "good old Northampton, and I'm off home for a few days to see her". Well he was a frequent visitor

134

after this, as he was stationed near Nottingham with the R.A.F. He asked me out to a dance, and the rest is history, for we fell in love and married and have lived happily ever after. Now, as an old couple, we look around us at the world today and sometimes wonder if it was all worth while. We all made so many sacrifices in the war, but we did all care about one another, so unlike today, when the young people only worry about themselves, and don't give a damn about us old 'uns.

I do thank you, Mr Bentinck, for what you do to fly the flag for us old 'uns.

Yours faithfully,
Margaret Drake.

Authors Reply:
Dear Margaret, Thank you so much for taking time to drop me a line and for telling me a little of your wartime story. I wonder just how many of us reading your story can remember watching those sweeps brushes coming out of the chimney ready to run and tell dad we can see them. It certainly brought back to me the memories of the times I watched for my father. I want you to know that I and so many others do appreciate what your generation gave and sacrificed for us younger ones to have a life today. Perhaps we can all take on board what you say and try even harder to educate our young people of what they owe to you, and also to care more for one another.
Yours most sincerely,
Michael Bentinck.

Letter from Mrs Sylvia Hollis, Lancaster.....

Dear Michael,
It was so good to hear you again on BBC Radio Lancashire on VJ Day. I think the way you speak of your late father and his comrades is just so wonderful. They really must be very proud of the way you fly the flag for them. If only the governments felt as you did, then I feel sure these brave heroes would have received a sincere apology and the

compensation that they so richly deserve long before now. Please don't give up now, Michael. Keep your letters going to the Prime Ministers, Presidents and Ambassadors of this world, as I know you do, and let's hope, before it's too late for these brave men, that our own Prime Minister will make sure that the Japanese compensate them at last. I believe that then, and only then, can Japan be reconciled, for the horrific treatment that they administered to our boys.

The part I played in World War II was nothing compared to what they did for King and country, but as you said you wanted to know what us women did for the war effort I thought I would send you an amusing tale that I took part in, during my Land Army days.

Once I joined the Women's Land Army, it was goodbye to London for me and farewell to city life, for it was now the country life for me, and all that went with it. I thought the smell of the smogs of London could be bad in the thirties and forties, but when some of those farmyard smells hit your nostrils, it near made one reach. I was sent to work on many of the farms around Cambridgeshire, and was billeted in hostels at Willingham and Swavesey, two nearby villages. From here we were taken to farms around the area where we did all manner of farm work – I even learnt to plough a field and drive a tractor, which made a nice change from working on crop picking, and when it came to sugar beet.... that was a real back killer, let alone the frostbite for your fingers. On one of the farms that I worked on the farmer really was a dirty old man, and I don't think his wife even got on with him, which made it worse for us girls. I won't mention any names, for it would not be fair to his wife, and she was a smashing person, as was the farmer if he hadn't had such a dirty mind. He was always making improper suggestions to us girls, and today I suppose he would be had up for sexual harassment. One day it was so very hot, and we had been working on making up a hay stack. He, of course, was working bare-chested, and to be honest we all kept complaining of how hot we were, when he said "go on with you, take your tops off and let the sun to your body, plus you will feel cooler". Well, one of the girls was daft enough to do it! She was a well built girl, and I would say had at least a 38" bust. She kept her bra on of course, but as she worked, we other girls could see how excited the farmer was getting. We told her not to be daft and put her top back on, to which the farmer shouted out "I don't mind looking at your breasts love" and with that he ran up to her and touched her breasts. She screamed of course, and although us others were very shocked, we ran and pulled him off of her. Well, we all decided it was time to teach him a lesson, so, as we outnumbered him six to one, we stripped him off and tied him to an old metal pole that was concreted in the middle of the field. I think the pole was used to tie the scarecrow to, and I remember one of the girls saying he would make a good scarecrow even if he is naked. When it was time to finish work we still left him there and went back to the farmyard to be collected. His wife asked us where he was and we told her he had not been with us, and that we thought we had heard him shouting in the bottom field. She said "oh well, he'll come home when he's ready for his tea". As we left to go back to the hostel we told our driver what had happened and he said "good for you, girls. Teach the dirty old git a lesson". Well, the next morning as we drew into the yard, he came to us and said "girls, please don't say anything to the Mrs or anyone about yesterday", then he rushed inside. Of course we didn't say anything to his wife, or anyone else on the farm but he never joined us for work that day or for the next few days. Thankfully he was never any more trouble to us girls from that day on. A few days later I was in the farmhouse speaking with his wife, when she said "what do you make of my old man then?" I hesitated with my reply as I didn't want to upset her, but before I could answer she said, "the other day when I asked you girls if you had seen him.... well, you were right – he was in the meadow all right, but you'll never guess what he was doing.... he was only sun bathing in the nude, and the reason he hasn't been back to work with you is because he's only gone and got his old man badly sunburnt. Well I've told him he needs looking at, a man of his age sunbathing in the nude. Whatever does he think he's doing, it must be his time of life". Well, when I got back to the fields and told the other girls, we all had a good laugh I can tell you, as I have many times since when I reflect on that time in my life, but, as I say, he never bothered us again and I think he learnt the lesson that us Land Army girls were not to be messed with.

I enjoyed my time working on the farms in and around Cambridgeshire, and the people were very kind to us in our dig for victory. We all had to suffer much at that time – the work was hard and the hours were long, but we never had to suffer like your father and his comrades – at least we had a warm dry bed to sleep in and good food to eat. As you know, Michael, I went on to marry a Far Eastern Prisoner of War, and although he died young at 48 years of age through what he suffered in the war, he was a kind and loving husband to me, and it was a pleasure to make his life that bit better for him in any way I could. He was a Lancashire lad and like so many others gave and suffered so much for King and country, that it makes what us ladies did seem like nothing, but I thank you, Michael, for the part you are playing in telling the world of what we ladies did. I send you and your family my very

Best Wishes,

Mrs Sylvia Hollis.

Our last letter covers a different kind of war time woman, but one who played such a vital part for the future generation of our great country. The gentleman who sent me the following was an evacuee, and as the next book I plan to write will relate some of the true stories of what evacuees went through in World War II, I felt it appropriate to finish this, my fourth book, with his letters to me describing his memories of his young wartime days. Also, as this book has been one of ladies' stories, I think it is appropriate to show what an important part women played in taking evacuees into their homes. I know my own mother, who in World War II lived at home with her parents in the village of Impington, Cambridgeshire, where I live today, took in two evacuees – a boy, Ralph, and a girl, Marigold, both of whom had come from London. Marigold was Jewish, and her family had been lucky enough to escape from Hitler's grip on Europe and get to London. I dare say they lived in fear every day though, knowing that he only had to cross that English Channel. Little Marigold stayed with my mother and grandparents throughout the war, as did Ralph, who, my mother tells me, was a proper boy and always in trouble, even found once playing with an unexploded bomb in the fields behind my grandparent's house. He thought it was great fun and like all children could not see any fear at all, and wondered why the adults were making such a fuss. They became lifelong friends of my grandparents, and I myself remember as a child going to London with my mother and father to visit Marigold and her parents, a Mr and Mrs

Adleman. I remember Mr Adleman was blind, and as a child it would frighten me when he would feel all over my eyes and face before saying "hello, Michael". Of course, today I know why he did this. I could also see how grateful they all were to my family for caring for Marigold through those war years.

I hope you will find the following evacuees' memories of interest, and if you have an evacuee story to tell please do drop me a line if you would like your story told in print for future generations to know of.

Letter from Mr and Mrs Roy Hattersley, Harlow, Essex.....

Dear Michael,

My wife, Pam, and I have heard you a few times now on radio, and always enjoy your wartime stories. I think it fair to say that the best programme we have heard you on is BBC Radio Cambridgeshire, with your presenter friend Mandy Morton. Like you, Mandy has time for her listeners, and when you are on together you trigger off such wonderful memories from the older listeners about their wartime experiences. I was only aged seven in 1939, so my memories are so different from those men and women who gave so much for our today. When I heard you last with Mandy, you mentioned that you would be writing a book on "WAR TIME WOMEN". Well, I would like to tell you about one wonderful lady who cared for my sister and I in World War II for yes, we were evacuees.

We were sent from our home in Chingford to a village called Birch, near Colchester in Essex. We were taken in by Mr and Mrs Smith who were so kind and caring towards us, for, as you will know, times were hard for all of us. But to be taken away from your home and family, as you can imagine, is so very hard for a child. For many evacuees it was to scar them for life – you must remember that not all were cared for as well as Mrs Smith cared for us. She really was a second mother to us, and did all she could to make us feel happy. She was no spring chicken herself, but she found energy from somewhere and did her best to keep us amused. I remember the co-op butcher's van called twice a week and would stand on the village green where we would walk with Mrs Smith to get the meat. Oh, my mouth still waters at the thought of the lovely creations she turned that meat into – home made steak and kidney pie, shepherds pie, meat pudding etc. It was only a small place that we were at – Hardy's Green, Birch, but when I think what it could have been like.... I know how much my sister and I owe to Mrs Smith. My sister was only 5 years old but we played well with the other kids, and I remember one day while playing in the village ditch I lost my wellington boot. I was so scared at what would happen, but Mrs Smith was so very good about it, and said "as long as you are all right, that's all that matters. We can soon get another wellington boot but we can't get another you, Roy".

I recently had an article published in the Essex Countryside Magazine asking if anybody knew of the Smith Family of Hardy's Green, Birch, near Colchester, whom we were billeted with as evacuees in 1939.

I received three very welcomed letters – one lady and one gentleman who wrote to tell me that they lived and grew up at Hardy's Green at roughly the same time as my sister and myself.

Hardy's Green was a small hamlet – a dozen cottages and a general shop. I was only 7 years old at the time and my sister was 5. I cannot remember everything that took place during the six months we stayed at Birch. My first memories with reference to the war was that my father joined the Royal Air Force as a volunteer reserve in Balloon Barrage at Chigwell in Essex. After his day's work for the Council he would dress up in his airman's uniform and cycle off from Chingford to Chigwell in the evening to do his bit pre-war.

Next, we all stood round the wireless at 11.15am awaiting Neville Chamberlain's speech saying, "We are now at war with Germany."

That self-same afternoon, my aunt arrived with two big canvas bags (made from deckchair canvas) for us to put our belongings in. Again, on that same afternoon (late), we arrived at Birch School, near Colchester on a double-decker bus and assembled in the main hall waiting to be billeted out with a family (didn't things move fast).

Looking back, I believe because we were a boy and girl, it seemed that we were almost the last to be chosen.

We arrived at the Andrews' farmstead late that evening and shown to our bedroom. This is where the canvas bags come in. In the bag, besides our belongings, I suppose a change of clothes, a tin of corned beef, some biscuits, toothpaste and a bar of Lifebuoy soap. Because the bar of soap had sweated all day in the bag, the smell of the soap as I placed it on the washstand will live with me forever.

There we were in a strange place, what was happening to us? Once we had explored the surroundings the next day, we found out that one of the barns had a goat in it which they used to milk for household use. The hay and farmyard smells one seemed to forget, and we settled down.

Mr Andrews was the shepherd for the main farmer, Gardner Church, so the main livestock was sheep. Mr Andrews gave me a shepherd's crook of my own and I went into the fields with him and tried to hook one, but I don't think I ever did catch one. I'm sure it was his way of trying to make me feel at home, bless him.

Then it seemed overnight we were re-billeted with the Smith family, for what reason I don't know to this day.

There we stood in this cottage front room (there was only one room downstairs), about 5.00pm in the evening, wondering what on earth had happened to us. Mr Smith was sitting in a chair by the fire range with a smile on his face. We soon began to love the Smiths.

It was only a small cottage, one of three in a block. The Smith's was on the end – one room downstairs and two bedrooms. It had a very long garden and the water came from the well and a rainwater butt. The toilet was down a very long garden, quite a long walk in the middle of the night. I remember the seat had two holes in it, all the contents were used on the garden (what rhubarb!). I went there in the middle of the night only to be greeted by the cat who had had her newborn kittens in there.

I don't remember very much about my school days, only the long walk to school, two miles from the Andrews'. I have since clocked it in my car, it is perhaps one and a half miles from the Smith's. My sister always asked for a piggy back ride on the way home. As you can imagine, I wasn't too pleased!

Also the very long winter.... the snow drifts seemed to reach right up to the sky on the high banks at the sides of the lane and when it started to thaw, the water and ditches were in full flood, sights never to be forgotten.

One morning on the way to school, one of the local lads said "I wonder how deep the water is in the ditch". I put my foot in and the rush of water swept my wellington boot right off of my foot and disappeared into a culvert never to be seen again.

Looking back, the Smiths were a wonderful couple. Sam's

141

occupation was an Essex roads man. I'm sure he had a horse and tip cart and a stretch of road and ditches to maintain. He brought me home my first catapult prongs from the hedgerow. Mrs Smith worked in a big farmhouse and the owner used to allow Sam to shoot-trapnetsnare rabbits and shoot pigeons on his land, and on many occasions he took me with him. He had approximately twelve ferrets in hutches in the garden and of course always took a couple in a sack when rabbitting. I saw him pick off a rabbit with his 12 bore as it bolted across the field. The empty cartridge had a smell to remember.

The village bobby used to call at the cottage on Saturday nights for his Sunday lunch.

My sister used to go with Mrs Smith to Colchester on a Saturday afternoon, whilst I was with Sam rabbitting. Mrs Smith would put my sister Olive on the back of her bike and ride to a point where she would catch the bus. She left her bike in the hedgerow and it would still be there when she came back (I don't think you would be so lucky today). The only time I went with her I got lost in Woolworths (plenty of tears).

The BBC Radio broadcast a programme during the 50th Anniversary called "No one cried when the last train pulled out" which featured Michael Aspel and Henry Cooper to name but two. One of the stories made reference to the cruelty of selection. People were picking children from the back of a lorry, and on the tailboard was a boy named Teddy Cook. They said no one would pick Teddy – he was small with jam jar bottom glasses. All of a sudden somebody said "I'll take him", and he jumped off of the tailboard. No sooner had his feet touched the ground when they said "Oh no, I'll have the twins". Teddy had the last laugh, he went to a nice family and the twins burnt down the barn where they were billeted.

The Parish News and the school logbook entries capture our stay at Birch School. Because there were so many children, all of a sudden the school had to operate a shift system, be it mornings or afternoons, to accommodate local children and evacuees.

With reference to the snowball blocking the road, Pat told me that when the village of Hardy's Green was cut off, children pulled sledges down to the school to get supplies for the village which they enjoyed doing. So when the snow-plough got through it made them redundant, so they rolled this great big snowball off the surrounding hilly fields to block the road again.... one could say, "Happy Days".

Also the entry reference "Head Lice" – the nurse's visit to the church hall to inspect our heads.... none in mine, of course!

Michael, as you said, folk who gave homes to evacuees must have been a special breed, as I am sure there must have been problems on both sides. Having said that, I think it left a lasting fondness for the folk who took us in.

I was still at work when the 50th anniversary came around and as it grew near I used to exchange stories with other work colleagues and they all had this urge to revisit their old haunts like Cornwall and Wales, where they were evacuated.

There must be endless stories to be told, like the family of five boys from London who went to the big manor house at Oxford and slept in white sheets for the first time in their lives. They had been used to sleeping five to a bed at home. Now they had a bed of their own.

They stayed there for approximately four years and when they eventually went home nothing had changed.... the front door key still hung on the same piece of string. So sad for them, back to no sheets again. The same old house that they had left four years ago, after all that luxury of the manor house!

Also, a gentleman at work told me the story of when he was evacuated in a remote part of Cornwall, near Helston. He said one week that they used to play a game of bagatelle in the front room with only oil lamps for lighting.

He said one Sunday night "can we play bagatelle" and the room went silent. All of a sudden the man of the house said "Bagatelle, on a Sunday," and repeated "Bagatelle, on a Sunday". He thought "what have I done?" It has lived with him, his memory of the look of horror on their faces in the flickers of the oil lamps.

I used to visit the Smith's over the years while they were alive and they always made us very welcome. One visit, after Mrs Smith passed away, Queenie, the daughter asked us in and sat us down on the settee. She then said "I ain't got you." I said, "I'm Roy the evacuee", she said "oh the little evacuees". (What trust).

To round this up, I also enclose photos of both our VE street parties, mine at Hawkdene, Chingford, and Pam's at Manor Farm Drive, Chingford.

I hope this gives a picture of our stay at Birch of which I have very fond memories.

I also think it's like when you did National Service, you remember the good times but not the bad.

I do realise that you can't use all of this but as Richard would say "you did try though".

Michael, I think the last words reference evacuees at Birch must come from the School Log Book.....

1940

May 22nd   Visit of Dr Alderton in connection with diphtheria immunisation of evacuated children.

May 29th   All Government evacuees are to be removed to another area. Visit of Dr Alderton for a medical examination of Government evacuees.

June 2nd   Sunday Government. Evacuees left the district at 07.30hours morning.

June 21st   School closed at the end of the afternoon session for two week's pea and fruit picking.

Michael, they left almost as fast as they arrived, I wonder where they went? I had already gone home so I didn't witness the scene.

Bye for now.
Best wishes to Hilary and your goodself.
Yours sincerely,
Roy and Pam Hattersley

Well my friends, we have now come to the end of our journey through this book. I really do hope it has been a worthwhile trip for you all. You have met just a few of my dear Land Army heroes, but before we finish please do allow me to share just a small story with you that two real heroes of mine were involved in regarding the Women's Land Army. The two heroes are my own dear late father, and my own dear mother. Firstly, though, allow me to tell you about two other ladies who have inspired me to write this book.

While researching this book I was so pleased to meet and receive letters from so many dear Land Army Girls, that of course I was overflowing with the excitement of it all. I wanted so much to tell some of these stories to people and see what their reaction would be to give me some idea if the stories would go to make a good book. After I had shared them with my wife Hilary, she too couldn't wait for the ladies' letters to come in and we would sit and read through them together and yes, like me, she thought they were good enough to include in a book. I then tried them on my dear friend Mandy Morton, a presenter and producer with BBC Radio Cambridgeshire. Mandy thought them so good that we did some programmes together and mentioned some of the stories that I had to date. This really opened the flood gates and thankfully so many people wrote to Mandy and I with their wartime stories, that this book has been able to be published.

The other lady I tried them on was my own mother. It was in November 1997 as I drove my mother to fly off to Singapore with another Far Eastern Prisoner of War widow, on a trip arranged by the Royal British Legion. She and the party she was to fly with, wanted to mark remembrance week by being near to where their dear husbands suffered so much. As we drove along we spoke of World War II, and my mother told me how, at 14years of age in 1937, she left school. The school today is known as Histon Infants School, but in the 1930s of course, it was the village school. My grandparents told my mother "if you are leaving school Dulcie, you better find yourself a job", so the day before she left school she called in at Chivers factory on her way home from school and asked if she could have a job. She was told "be here at 7.30am tomorrow, please". Yes, mum had got her first job and as she told me this I thought to myself "oh, if only it was so easy for the youngsters of today to find a job". Well of course when war broke out there she was on the production line at Chivers, on the jellies. She told me how she and the other girls often ate the jelly cubes – to them they were like sweets. She told me of nights at the Dorothy Dance Hall and the Rex in Cambridge, where she met my late father, and she recalled for me the day he said goodbye to her when he went off to the Far East, where he was never to forget the name of Singapore. She told me how she wished he could have been with her now to go back under better circumstances. I remember I said "come on mum, don't cry. Dad would be so pleased to know you were going. Why not tell me something amusing about your time at Chivers in the war?" She replied, "well you just imagine about five or six hundred of us girls coming out of the factory on our bikes at lunch time, for our 1 hour break. As you know, the railway station is just up the road from the factory, and you could bet your bottom dollar that the gates would be shut for a train to come through. All the girls would be moaning and would be fighting to get through the little side walkway gate before the train came. This caused so much commotion that in the end the station master locked the gate shut so that we had to wait, which always took 15 minutes off your lunch break, although really in those days we called it our dinner break. When the man did open the railway gates it was everyone for themselves – it was just a sea of bikes. I only lived half a mile from the factory on Cambridge Road, Impington, but many of the girls had to go right into Cambridge, so time was everything to them. I remember every day we had suet puddings – one day it would be as a meat pie, or stew and dumplings, then the next day it would be jam roly poly, or syrup pudding. It really was filling though, and so very good. It was then back on your bike and rush back to clock in before the buzzer went at 2.00pm. I remember the girls coming round on the delivery bike with pies etc for sale, which was much appreciated by those girls who came by train and bus from places like St Ives and Ely".

"At Impington College we had soldiers billeted and they would come to the factory to have their showers. Well, we worked just next door to this shower block and one of the girls drilled a hole through the wall and once all these soldiers were taking their showers, we girls took it in turn to watch them. We would call to one another 'oh, look at this one – he's a real ginger tom', or 'my goodness, he's a big boy'. I am sure you can imagine what us giggly girls were like, and once the lads came out of the showers we would go outside and chat to them, but they never did find out that we had been watching them".

146

I, of course, said "mother, may you be forgiven".

Perhaps you were a soldier who took his shower at that time in Chivers factory... well now, my friends, you know what these young girls were up to! My mother told me that my grandparents had open house most nights when these army boys would call in for something to eat and drink, and to have a chat and play cards. My mother told me that once she said to her mum, "you shouldn't keep cooking and doing so much for these soldiers mum", to which her mum replied, "Dulcie, would you not like to think that wherever your dear Jim is, that someone is cooking him a nice meal and making him feel more at home?" My mother never questioned her mum about it again for in the four years my dad was a prisoner of the Japanese, she only received one small card from him, which said 'I am well and working for pay'. As we now know, this really was a lie but at the time my mother hoped that someone was feeding him well. She told me when she did at last see him again in late 1945 she had a job to recognise him, for he still only weighed six stone, and when she had said goodbye to him all those years before he had weighed nearly 14 stone. As she said, it was like meeting a stranger and of course the Jim I had known as that young happy-go-lucky lad had changed into a very frightened young man, and it took him many years to slowly come back to me.

Here again I must thank all you wonderful ladies who, like my own mother, have been there for your husband and have helped him through his nightmares of those horrific days for them – you alone will know what real heroes they are, and I tell you here our country will never be able to repay them for what they gave for our today.

I go on record here to say that every government since World War II has not stood up for them as they should have, whatever political party has been in power. I feel they have let these men down by not demanding a sincere apology and compensation for them from the Japanese.

My mother went on to tell of a bad air raid that took place one day, when the German bombs fell on the fruit pulp barrel store. This was at the bottom of Poplar Road in Histon, where today there are houses. She told me the mess was everywhere and asked me to imagine this sticky fruit pulp all over the road and the nearby houses. I think the best story she told me, though, is this one, as it is of my own father and the Land Army girls....

147

Well, once my father was feeling much better in 1946 he got a job driving for the war agriculture department, where he had the job of driving the Land Army girls from their hostels to the farms etc. By now he had been married to my mother for a few months, and they rented a small cottage in Impington. My dad started very early in the morning and around 8.00am would call home for breakfast. On one such morning when he called home my mum was in the kitchen and didn't see my dad come in. He shouted "it's only me love, and is it alright if I bring my mate in for breakfast?" My mum replied "of course you can love. You both sit down and I will cook extra and bring it through". "Well", she told me, "when I came through into the room with the two breakfasts, I thought to myself 'I'll give him 'can I bring my mate in',' for he only had this blue-eyed blonde girl sitting beside him. I can assure you, Michael, when he came home later I gave him what for. I asked him if all the girls he was working with were like her, to which he replied 'yes love, most of them are'. I didn't want to appear to seem jealous for I loved him so very much, but I can see now why he loved the job so much, but after some of the people he had to drive around in the war, and what he had been through I'm glad that he found such a happy job for himself and I know it was a sad day for him when the Land Army disbanded".

Once I had said my goodbyes to my mother as she set off for the Far East, I drove home thinking to myself how lucky I have been not to have known the real heartache of war, like my own mum and dad and so many of you have. I gave thanks to God that I had been born in 1949 and had been able to grow up in the 50s and enjoyed my teenage years in the swinging 60s. I know enough of history to know that each century has its best parts to be born in, and I know that I was born in what I think is the best part of this century. I can remember my childhood growing up in Histon in the 50s when you never had to worry about locking your doors, and of how everyone helped one another – such happy days. I also know what a great mum and dad I had to love and care for me and to use one of my dads sayings, "I was one of the lucky ones". Perhaps one day I will write a book on my own life, for I know my childhood memories could fill a book, like the time I tied my dads old Austin Seven to the back of the coalman's lorry while he delivered our sacks of coal, and when he drove out of our driveway dad's car followed him out and in to the ditch across the road. I think it fair to say I kept out of the way for a while after that, but mum and dad soon forgave me for they really were loving caring parents, and if you have read my other books you won't need me to tell you how very proud I am of them. I am also so very proud of all you wonderful people who gave so much in World War II, so that I could have a life today. I know I have said this before and will say it again, but if you dear brave people had not answered the call of King and country, and Nazi Germany and the Japanese had won the war, I don't believe for one minute that I would have been able to enjoy the life that I have had.

So many of you have written to me to say how moved you were with my other books. You say "I cried, I laughed, but couldn't put the book down". Well, my friends, I hope this book has had the same effect on you, and until the next book I wish you all a fond farewell.

CLARENCE HOUSE
SW1A 1BA

11th December 1997

Dear Mr. Bentinck,

        Queen Elizabeth The Queen Mother sends
you and your wife her best wishes for Christmas
and the New Year, and thanks you for your
remembrance of Her Majesty.

        As with the many other kind messages
the Royal Family have received this year,
The Queen Mother much appreciates these
greetings at Christmas time.

        Her Majesty, who was interested to learn
of the books you have written as well as the one
you are now writing, hopes that you too will
have a Happy Christmas and New Year.

                Yours sincerely,

                Margaret Rhodes

                Lady-in-Waiting

M. J. Bentinck, Esq.,

GRANDFATHER'S WAR
by Andrea Hoyland
July 1995

It's fifty years since '45, when we were told "it's over",
But it wasn't all that easy, we weren't rolling in the clover.
Vivid memories stay with us, you can hear them recount tales,
Even of the war at home when the siren starts to wail.
The R.A.F. took off at dusk, just as the sun was setting.
Wives looked up, and saw them leave – another night of fretting.
Dawn brought them straggling back, first a bomber then a fighter,
Lancaster and Wellington all landed so much lighter.
Hurricane and Spitfire had led them to their quarry,
Where they dropped their awful load, that was not much worry,
But now they had to turn around and run the gauntlet back,
Through Jerry's planes and searchlights and try to miss the flack.
Ground crews stood looking at the sky and listening for the drone
Of each one coming in and landing at the drome.
Sometimes one would burst in flames, another missed the runway,
While one ran into sandbags and they heard the pilot say,
"The damn thing's like a colander, how did I get it here?.
You've got ten hours to patch her up, so get out all your gear".
Mechanics worked on engines and the body crews arrived
With pots of glue and brushes, to help the planes survive.
They pasted fabric over holes, along the body and the wings.
Dad said it reminded him of the Walrus with his "sealing wax and string'
When the day was over, they were fit again to fly
And though the paint was still quite wet, they rose into the sky.
Each man in every service could relate to you his tale,
In fact, each man could write a book, but there wouldn't be much sale.
World War Two is written down in some history books
And can be found on library shelves, should you care to look.
But you won't find the grief and tears of a generation there.
I just hope Grandad wrote it down and then perhaps you'll care.
Yes, 1945 was the year that peace descended,
But many had to stay abroad with just a stone up-ended,
To try and tell the world of grief a war can cause.
So each November stand in church and for a moment pause,
To think of those who died for us, so we could all be free,
And those who came home ill and lame and those who cannot see.